Shades
of Black
and Blue

a collection of poetry

BW4C

Thank you for your support
May God Bless ♡
No doubt
BW4C

aBM

Published by:
A Book's Mind
PO Box 272847
Fort Collins, CO 80527
www.abooksmind.com

In Loving Memory of my child

Acknowledgements

Thanking first GOD who is the head of my life.

Thanking forward, my writing partner JJ: If it wasn't for her I wouldn't have the editing done. Thanking A BOOKS MIND publishers, graphics, formatters and everyone who helped to get this together and published. Thanking my Writers Group, for listening and helping to get this book in order. Thanking BJC for her editing expertise. Thanking Sojourner House for their endorsements. Thanking ALL of my SUP-PORTERS, whether it was MONEY, ENCOURAGEMENT, ACCEP-TANCE, An OPPORTUNITY To SPEAK, FOOD, A SHOULDER TO LEAN ON, or WHATEVER else GOD Laid on Your Hearts to do FOR ME, With All of my Heart, With All of MY LOVE, With All of MY Mind, I am GRATEFUL To GOD for YOU!!!!!! HALLELUJAH!!!!

The Seed

Matthew 13:24-30
Be careful of the Seeds you Plant

MOMMA

Throw-Away Child

This girl-child of mine
I did not want to make
Her life, her Father won't let me take

Stuck in a marriage I did not want,
My caregiver set up this taunt

"He loves me," he says
I'm not his first, no amends

If this were a boy instead,
I wouldn't wish the child dead

For then, I'll be the first in his life
Instead of this man's whatever numbered wife

The girl-child I did not want to make
I'll see to it her life in Hell to bake

FATHER

A Child to Love

For the longest time I believed
That men gave birth to girls,
And women gave birth to boys
That's how it must be

'Cause my dad was the only one who loved me so
It wasn't 'til much later
That my grandmother came along
Did her best to teach me a new song
But for me somehow, I still didn't belong

For no matter what my dad had to do
His love for me always came through

It wasn't 'til I had seen several live births
That I truly understood
How I really got to this earth

My dad was always special to me
He filled my heart with joy, pain, and glee

No Choice No Voice

Age four (4) first fall down
In the middle of the street looking around

Mother pissed as hell
Looking for attention, to everyone she did tell

What hope can be gained
If I'm one large blood stain

Not able to move
Had to find another groove

Leaning to the right doing a slow drag crawl
My grandmother snatched me up like a rag doll

She stopped traffic just like that
Missing a car that would have laid me flat

Mother took my voice
Feeling rejected my only choice

I Disappear

I Disappear
I used to see what I looked like as a baby
My pictures are going away
My little brother's are here to stay

I disappear
Slowly, but surely, my pictures are replaced
My little brother's cover them even spaced

I disappear
I no longer exist
There's no more room for me a new twist

I disappear
Nothing I do is right
I'm told I'm stupid no longer bright

I disappear
Little by little 'til there is nothing left
I'm sad don't know what to do
Don't know who I am

I disappear
Even my birthday isn't my own
I have to share the day with little brother I moan

Here at what is called a home, I disappear

Christmas

It's Christmas what do I see
No toys for me
Everything is for little brother
'Cause he belongs to Mother
It's starting to sink into my brain
Not only do my pictures disappear,
But nothing including Christmas is the same
Mother said she didn't want a girl
Especially after I stood on Dad's feet
Danced and did a twirl,
She said I'm an attention-getting brat
Even when in corners I sat
She didn't want a girl first
Especially in the month of my birth
I was really mad,
Now I'm just sad
Nobody is supposed to love me
I'm bad, selfish, stubborn, and stupid
You see

Knees vs Eyes

Three years later, I'm seven now
My baby brother is three, and his eye goes *POW*!

Meanwhile I'm continuing to fall
Not feeling like I've grown at all

I fall downstairs
I fall upstairs

I fall at the sink
I fall in the street, don't have to think

Lots of physical pain
Loss of emotional gain

Yelled at, hit more, I can't tell
Wish someone would ring the end bell

Attention-Getting Slut I'm called
When all I did was fall

Then the boy she wanted
His eye starts taunting

A choice was made
Get him fixed right away

Can't say what about me
'Cause mother will laugh with glee

So I continue to be broken
Like a slug instead of a token

His eye won out
Pain shoots through my knee, but I can't cry out

HAIR

Pull, yank, slap,
Pull, yank, slap,
That's the rhythm of the hair tap
Hold still you brat
I said I never wanted a girl, and I meant that
Finally going to a relatives house
Although I try to be quiet as a mouse
The relative looks at me
Come here can I comb her hair
This she asks of my mother
She's tender-headed I don't care she's a bother
Come here sweetheart the relative says
I look back at my dad who nods his head
Sitting on the floor, I flinch as she picks up the comb
"It's okay," she soothingly whispers in my ear
I promise not to hurt you my dear
Slowly she parts my hair, puts in sections with a clip
Whispering words of gentleness and love
For the first time feels like heaven above
She parts the first section further, greases the scalp
Softly and tenderly, I feel like I can fall out
She then calls over my mother
She has soft easy hair,
It doesn't take much care
If you take your time and do it right,
She'll fall asleep on your lap each night
Instead of taking it as kind advice
My mother gets mad, says I embarrassed her
Made her look bad,
Is my attention-getting butt finally glad
She never takes the relative's advice

Pull, yank, slap,
Pull, yank, slap,
That's the rhythm of the hair tap
Till I can do it on my own at 16
Getting my hair done was mean

Not allowed

Wasn't allowed to touch my little brother
He belongs to Mother
Could not brush his hair
I'm bad 'cause I say not fair
Can't hold him, talk to him
Look at him or try to be a big sister
Then I start to disappear picture by picture

Not allowed to hug my own dad
'Cause he lights up happy and glad
He knows how to make me laugh
He was teaching me how to dance
He brought me pretty clothes that fit
He said I was pretty his baby girl
Then he turned me around in a twirl
He brought me gifts every now and then
We ate together until I said when
None of that is allowed any more
There's nothing I can say or do, Mother is a chore

Not allowed to feel, to cry, to just be
I'm chained up can't be free
No expressions can I have
No voice, no choice
No friends that I chose
Nothing new, nothing that fits
I can't trade and play with other girls' dolls
Accused of stealing, just because
No nail polish with pretty colors
Can't ask questions 'bout life
No dreams for me 'bout being a wife

Not allowed to explore my world
To dream, to think, to figure out what I'd like to be
No favorite color, food, fashion for me

Not allowed to have a mind of my own
Go where I want to go
Express an opinion
No support, protection for me
'Cause it's not allowed, you see

Glasses

I couldn't see, but what could I do
It would be another reason to get me beat blue

So I say nothing to anyone but my teacher
Who made me sit closer to the board, like a preacher

Finally, a heavy rain came down
I could see nothing in town

Couldn't see my dad who was supposed to pick me up
Tears running down my face I shook

Finally deciding to walk home
Soaking wet, needed a hair comb

Looking towards the house
It was quiet as a mouse

Walked right on by
To a neighbor's house while I cried

Finally, Dad found me
With no questions or explanations, he beat me while I screamed I
couldn't see

Within twenty-four hours, my teacher sent home a note
"Your child can't see," she wrote

Still not believing a word either of us said,
Mother tested my eyes herself instead

I couldn't see the box up on a shelf
No apology offered, no reparations made, but I was glad inside myself

For once again, I proved
That I wasn't lying or trying to get attention, but still I did not move

Finally to a doctor who did proclaim
Most definitely, glasses for this child you must claim

Abuse

Oh man, my life is of no use
Every day Momma finds some other excuse

To hit, kick, scream, and yell
Don't even need a bell
I'm a child—who am I gonna tell

No one would believe me anyway
What more could I say

My life really doesn't matter
Momma is crazier than a hatter

Poor dad doesn't have a clue
It's amazing how she gets him to beat me black and blue

If only he knew how well she lied
How much she wishes I'd just die

What can I do to stop this mess
What did I do to be a pest

Grandmother can't do much
Except on occasion, provide a loving touch

In school, I'm not even cool
The kids pick on me and try to use me as a tool

If only someone would come to my rescue
Get me out of this house
'Cause I'm scared to sleep always feeling like a louse

Constantly told I'm uglier than the dirt on the bottom of her shoes
All I want to do is come unglued

Most days I can't even think
My life really stinks

Help

Feeling lonely, black and blue
With the lies Mother tells, I get beat too

Don't know how much more I can take
Doing my best to ignore the pain, a smile I try to fake

Nobody wants to be my friend
Not even the ones in let's-pretend

I don't know what else to do
My days are shades of black and blue

Nana

Oh boy, only one week a year
I get to be someplace not so severe
A placed filled with love
It's my place like heaven above
Dad and I leave early for breakfast and I'm his baby girl
In the parking lot, he gives me a twirl
Dad and I share a plate
He checks his watch so not to be late
My nana is there arms open wide
Welcoming me inside
She takes me shopping for clothes that fit
We talk, laugh,
I watch her fire
Hear her wit
Then she gently combs my hair
Her bracelets jangle like music in my ears
I know she cares
Uncle goes to get the car
A garage near the house not far, three things are planned for me
A picnic, church, and a block party
I have fun, and real friends for a week
Nana doesn't scream—she speaks
She likes pond's cold cream
She shares with me, not mean
It's time for Dad to pick me up
Nana dresses me pretty, combs my hair into a puff
Dad lights up with a smile
My pretty baby girl
I giggle, give a twirl,
Dad drops into a pile
Scoops me up like it's been awhile

He puts me down
He and Nana talk
I say bye to Uncle, to the car we walk
Dad takes me to dinner
Hamburgers and fries a winner
As we head for what is called home
We both swallow, try not to groan
I know I won't get to wear the new clothes Nana bought
I try not to cry at the thought
I try not to think of the kids at school
Who are mean and cruel,
I try to hold on to my one week of good memories
As I stare out the window at trees
Slowly dad pulls in front the house
We have arrived
My only thought—I gotta try to survive

First Attempt

My one week a year is gone now
My nana lost her head somehow
This last year I went, I can tell something was wrong
She cried a lot, didn't know who she was, and I tried to be strong
My one week with real friends is gone
I'm stuck with mean people to no end
The pretty clothes I no longer get
The ones that don't fit I try to accept
Dad and I had one last fight
'Cause I'm tired of being beat for no reason every night
I'm tired of Mother's lies
Also her phony cries
Dad promised to never beat me again
Both he and I try to mend
I'm tired—I've had enough
Dean at school says I gotta be tough
All these thoughts run through my mind
As I look over the bridge the first time
Second time I throw my leg over
Just as I get ready to make the drop
Somebody I know yells stop
Where did they come from, there wasn't anybody near
I checked to make sure the coast was clear
They ran to tell Little Brother
He runs home tells Mother
When I get home, she snatches me up to her face
I blank out 'cause she's in my space
So you want to die
Why don't you jump next time
As she says those words
I think of another plan
I will not hesitate next time
It'll happen if I can

Discovery

A new kind of freedom at last
I realize buses go places, and don't just pass
A place I found I can hide
Until my father comes home to be at my side

Places full of books that make me laugh
I can then concentrate on my math
They have special classes there too
I can hide from the shades of blue

A class on poetry I took,
Writing things down helped relieve me
As my hands shook
My teacher liked one for a book

He submitted it first for a contest
In my district, it was the best
Then my writing my mother discovered
Beat me through the house every wall I covered

Made up for my dad another lie
Told him I'll kill him first before I die
Snatched the belt out of his hand
I'm tired of being beat for nothing I demand

We fought 'til we both grew tired
That's it he said, no more you're wired
No more beatings for you
'Cause I'll have to kill you next time that would make me blue

Meantime my poem made it to the state

No choice my mother and I had a date
As I accepted my award
With tears in my eyes, I threw the poem out when I leaned forward

Never will I write again
I plan my escape from this hell instead
At age 12 writing I did stop
For it did nothing more than make Mother blow her top

Safe Haven

Church is a good place
I can be me in GOD'S space
GOD used to talk to me
Now I feel HIM more when I sing
I actually have friends in there
To me they actually seem to care
In high school, I got to do more things
Dad was happy I had friends
Accepted JESUS publicly at seven
Mother said no baptism 'til eighteen
This is a safe haven

Second attempt

I'm tired of these mean kids
Who get away with everything,
They put stuff in my book bag
I gotta check it before I go home
They play mean tricks
Do stuff slick
One boy stared at me real hard
Stupidly I asked why
They asked him loudly, I sighed
He said I was uglier than a hallmark card
Of course I left class and cried
Then my best friend, handicapped and white,
Told me black students thought being with me wasn't right
He can't really defend himself
So he had to put our friendship on a shelf
Then things are worse at home
Mother throws stuff and makes Dad mad at me
But Dad won't beat me
I've had enough I got to leave this high school
I know the perfect tool
Went up on the roof top
Going over the side to drop
Right in front of the cafeteria so they can see
Exactly what they done to me
The principal sent someone up real fast
Grabbing the one hand left I didn't let go
Struggling they pulled me up
The principal looked at me
Asked where I wanted to be
A transfer to another school
Where these mean kids don't rule
I finished out that semester
Transferred to a new school that September

New School

This new school has classes galore
Not enough time to explore
Signed up for everything I could
As long as I didn't get home before Dad
'Cause Mother is always mad
I'm tired of ducking and dodging the things she throws at me
Tired of her screaming 'til it's her breath you see
Tired of her lies since Dad stopped hitting me
The counselors here
Act like they care
They noticed I won't go home
The classes I took not to roam
They sent me to a special group
We are all misfits like a troop
I know better than to say much of anything
The last adult who tried to help
Mother lied and they turned against me instead
A friendship I had went dead
The best part, it takes a while on the bus
I can be walking down the street as Dad turns the corner
He drives I walk so I'm not a goner
We come in the house the same time
No more of Mother's fictionist crimes
Can't wait to go to college
I just love knowledge
Tried to get my worker's permit
Mother won't sign, pitched a fit
Wanted to go away, work summer camp
Money is my freedom lamp
That's okay
I have to wait another day

Finally, I can sign my own permit
Can't wait 'til I get it, Mother is in a snit
Using a different address, it's waiting for me
At my Mom round the corner
We celebrated a little free
Wanted her to teach me to drive
Mother swears I won't survive
That's okay
I'll wait for another day
Tried being a nurse
It didn't work out, thought I'd burst
Turned to business co-op program
More things for me to explore and see
Working hard for my money
Student aid report said parents could afford to send me to college
Excited to go away for more knowledge
Got an offer before I graduated
A salary and paid education
Turned it down thought I was leaving the state
Wasn't going anywhere found out too late—
No one comes to see me graduate,
Mother's on vacation, couldn't be interrupted out of state
A lousy phone call from Dad
I can tell he's mad
Hear Mother in the background,
I hope she didn't think we were going to hang around
Went out got drunk
Danced on the back of my friend's trunk

Third Attempt

Hanging out with my friends
I'm sad, mad thinking 'bout the end
Need another plan
Got to get out of Mother's land
Can't think straight
Don't want to go to the house of hate
Everyone is having a good time
All I can think of is dirt and grime
Don't know why I think like I do
Not supposed to feel
All I can think of is shades of dark and navy blue
As my friends and I climb to the top
What if I don't stop,
I could walk out into the air
Doubt there could be time to spare
Last person to arrive is me,
Keep walking—soon you'll be free
Somehow, my friends sense something is wrong
Caught in mid-air like a note in a song
We can't make it through without you
My friends say
Don't think we didn't notice you're having a bad day
All I can do is cry
LORD why won't you let me die
My friends surround me in a group hug
They smash me like a bug
LORD you got till I'm twenty-five
I will find a way _**not**_ to survive

Gone

The lights in Dad's eyes stay gone
He struggles to get home
There is no love, no peace in this house
Mother's cyclone of terror is worse than the sight of a mouse
Nothing anybody but Little Brother does is right
Do my best to stay out of her sight
If I get home too early
Duck and dodge dance 'cause things are hurled at me
While she screeches and yells
Of course nobody is gonna tell
I have one safe place to stay
Until Dad comes home at the end of the day
I hurry to my room before he goes back out
Ears ringing as mother lies and shouts
Don't know how much more Dad and I can take
I feel for him in this mistake
My focus now is to get a job,
So I can get out of this house of sob
Some peace, some quiet, some freedom to explore and be
That's what I seek after for me

Make no sense

Why would someone who doesn't want me around
Do her best to keep me a prisoner in her town

That's okay, I'll work each day
Save up what I could on my pay

Finally, six months from high school grad date
I left the home of hate

Tried my best to go to school
Found out more money was needed, I lacked that tool

So I worked and paid my bills
No time for frills and thrills

This is how my story began
Just think what it did to me if your head swam

THE TARES

Matthew 13:24-30
"The seeds planted as a child have grown and are wild"

NEW WORLD

Man, I finally got out
I could kick my heels and shout
Got a job
So many lights and pretty things
A world that blinks and blings

There is so much I haven't tried
But it's okay
I'll just take it each day

My new place is drab
The woman a bit of a crab
But I can come and go
Without having to say so
Making enough to pay rent
Signed into college the rest spent
I've got to take good notes
For each lesson I learn
So much I don't know 'bout life
This new world has some strife
Working two and a half jobs
And eighteen credits at college
I'm grateful for knowledge
I have real friends I can hang with
Acceptance no longer a myth
I can get in where I fit in
Try to make sure no sin
So much on my mind
So much to do
Make sure get the bills paid
That much I know to be true

Enjoying this new world
With all its pretty things
That blinks and blings

Find me a new place
Like the new landlady
Try to live by her rules

Try to do what's right
Try to be out of sight
Got a different job
A new college too
Maybe I'll get to do what I want to do
Don't understand the difference
Between a boy and a man
They seem to follow me everywhere!
That includes home
My mind on other things, so I don't hear what they say—it roams
Okay what did I just agree to
Don't understand what I said
To make them spin their head
Don't really have the time
Gotta go, class's 'bout to start
What was that about my heart

This new world has a language I can't speak
Don't know what to say
I hope I don't look weak
So much to learn
But no time left to burn
Two jobs and eighteen credits at college
I'd rather deal with the knowledge

STUCK

How on earth did I get stuck
With a man I really don't want to be bothered with
It's like I've been hit with a truck
Tripped me outside of my classroom
I was running to get to my last job
And *ZOOM*!
I thought I knocked him down
BOOM!

Next thing I know
He shows up everywhere I go
I tried to set him up on dates
Either he wouldn't go or be late
I even told him 'bout the three-year rule
Three years and marriage are the terms
Thought he would run like he'd been burned
No such luck he's still everywhere I go, even at school

So I guess I'm stuck
With this man *YUCK*!
Don't know what to do
He's turning my world midnight blue
Why can't he understand I don't want him as my man
Even his family is nuts
I'm a good actress shucks!

This man got me thrown out of my place
I don't have anywhere to replace
Back to the home of hate
Dad's happy, Mother's mad, darn fate
She doesn't understand my jobs

Acts like I steal and rob
When my job makes me work late
I get a limo home, and a dinner with steak
Dad is happy to have me home
He doesn't want me to roam
But it seems I got no choice
Once again, I've lost my voice

Dude says move with my aunt
At first, it seems smart
Then next thing I know
He gets a job where I go
He forgot to tell me
That he also has his aunt's keys

Now I really don't have space to think about finding a new place
We ride the train together
It don't matter the weather
I can't get away from him
He's everywhere without a whim
Why couldn't Mother leave me alone
To figure things out so I find a new place to go

So now I'm stuck
With a man I don't want *SHUCKS*
Things get worse
A baby to nurse
He talks me into an abortion
Make it sound like a magic potion
I can't see what choice I have
I'm stuck

Don't know what to do
With all this midnight blue

Three years can't go by fast enough
I'm tired of this man's stuff
Finally, I get another job
I like this one
It's my private get-away
I told him at my old job he'll have to stay
But he still insists on going as far
Into work with me
All I get is thirty minutes free
It's not enough to come up with a new plan
LORD, I'm tired of this man
Three years is almost up
We'll see what he'll do then
My friends have good men
I'm probably not worthy of them
That's why I'm stuck

Finally, three years are up
Okay now what
Reminding him of my three year rule
Although I work and go to school
He actually gets a ring
It's the real thing
Then he talks to his crazy mother
She says he shouldn't bother
I tell him that's fine
We can break up for sure this time
At least we tried
I can find me a new place
In time, my memory from his head will erase
He says no that won't do
I will marry you
Being the great actress that I am,

Okay if that what you say
We'll try that way
He tells his _**wench**_ of a sister
We don't have money for a wedding day
Seeing an opportunity to make her look like she's the best
She'll pay for it another test
The truth for me *I* can afford a wedding day
But it will be a waste of my money okay
I tell him if we last ten years
We'll have a wedding without the arrears
I can't lie to GOD in church
The courthouse doesn't count
'Cause love this ain't about
I thought I did what I could
To prove to him together we are no good
Then he'll have no choice you see
But to set me free
Until then, I'm stuck

MIDNIGHT BLUE PART I

My world is midnight blue
It's my fault true
There was no one to rescue me
So I can't get free
Things go from bad to worse
Man what a curse
I'm glad I never really gave my heart
From the very start
Reality for him finally sets in
I'm paying big for this sin
He runs to his wench sister and mother
Midnight Blue: I have no money
Why does he even bother
Wench says she'll reset the budget
One problem with that
I make more than him *oh snap*!
They don't know I'm downstairs,
My voice sends them into fear
The problem is he doesn't want the responsibility
That comes with me
It's my money he wants
I told him if he can't be a man
He can leave fast as he can
Midnight Blue: Never mind, we're okay
Back at the house
He acts like a louse
He screams at me that it's not fair
For him to help around the house
I know for sure now he really don't care
I tell him to mop the floor
He calls his mother once more

Midnight Blue: Whose responsibility is it (he asks)
Hangs up my mother said it's your task
It's your wifely duty
Mine is your booty
Next, he complains about his job
He doesn't want to work
Swears it's because it's not enough money
Has the nerve to call me honey

The truth is he has no skills
He only attended college long enough
To get into the fraternity stuff
Sadly, the fraternity is stuck with him as well
Though they won't admit it and tell
He doesn't support, protect, or love me
He lets his family get him out of everything
I knew this marriage wouldn't last
Glad I didn't waste my money can't wait 'til this is past
He lets his family gang up on me
Blames me for everything
Find out I'm pregnant again
His **wench sister** and crazy mother says
I've forced him into marriage
Now a baby carriage
I say once again he can leave
Trust me there is no cleave
Midnight Blue: I want to stay
I want him to go away
Midnight Blue throws three hundred dollars at me
Don't come with it your body better be free

PROPHETIC PROMISE

Three doctors concluded measure for measure
Your body wasn't made for giving birth, but for pleasure

It's a good thing you got rid of the last one
You would have both died
Child smothered on the inside
You would have bled outside

The first one looked at me with a smirk
I hope for my sake your lawyer is a jerk
I asked why he spoke that way
'Cause death is the price for this pregnancy, you'll pay

The second one, a woman, came unglued
Whipped out a hankie and boo hooed
Now what's the matter with you
Death in this pregnancy she said is your due

Third doctor looked and smiled
God has taken me over worse miles
I'll do my best
This is a test
The question is *whose* death

I'll do what I can
To bring at least one of you into the is world, the best possible way
No promises okay

I liked him best
I went home and prayed about this test

Lord, I know this is a consequence of my marriage choice
Hear me out can I have a voice
If it is my child's death, let it be delayed
If it is mine, let me see him I promise not to stay

Lord said all right, I'll change the date
But eventually he'll meet his fate

Pound for pound, measure for measure
God created me not to give birth, but to give pleasure

MIDNIGHT BLUE PART II

Went shopping with his three hundred dollars while I cried
Know he'll be mad if I lied
Told him that I'm not getting rid of this child
He goes completely wild
He insists he'll stay
I know he'll find some way to make me pay
Does everything to make me miscarry
Starts fights, like I forced him to tarry
Tried talking to his friends
They says things will get better when the pregnancy ends
I want so badly to disagree
I can't, I have nowhere to be
Everybody is mad at me
Suddenly **Midnight Blue** claims he's found his dad
He'll leave with him after the baby I'm glad
I hurry and pack all his things
Leave it at the door, like it's got wings
Midnight Blue says he won't leave 'til the baby is born
On the inside I mourn
My dad says that's a mistake
He won't come back
I don't care, tired of the fights and hidden attacks
With this child he won't bond
Which is good 'cause this marriage is done

ANSWERED PRAYER

Big brown eyes that looked like mine
Except about the size of a dime

Yellow skin that would turn sugar brown
My child arrived alive, in a crazy world and town

It took a lot to bring him here
My child to rear

Thank you Lord for delaying his fate
I'm hoping you'll forget about the death date

WENCH

Name dropping, fake wanna-be that can't be
She's uncouth you see
She's a
Wench

Can't cook worth a dime
A waste of your time
She's a
Wench

She tells instant lies if you don't do things her way
She'll block your highway
She's a
Wench

A meddling instigator in your life
A contentious shrew of a wife
She's a
Wench

A controller, manipulator, who do anything for credit
Be careful your life she'll edit
She's a
Wench

The type you turn your lights out, so you look like you're not home
Don't answer your phone
It's da
Wench

She's lazy, crazy, and hates to be busted

Can't be trusted
You can get easily disgusted
By da
Wench

Have you seen her in a dress
Looks like a test
What a mess
She's a
Wench

We all know one
She's a son-of-a-gun
She's a
Wench

Keep this in mind
You'll find I'm not unkind
'Bout da
Wench

Quick and phony tears, she'll wail
So here's da tale of the
Wench

TRIBULATIONS

Two weeks after my child arrives
I'm glad, 'cause my child and I are alive
Midnight Blue says good-bye
So glad, I pretend to cry
I kick my heels and dance
With my child in my arms, I prance
Wench sister-in-law shows up out of nowhere
Sees me dance without a care
Oh, you lonely for my brother,
Please he's a bother
We get into a fight
I tell her get out of my sight
I get a phone call later
Midnight Blue yells at me
I'm shocked as can be
Wench sister called him and said
I threw my child across the room
Abused him in front of her, caused her gloom
My mouth opens wide
I scream at him like I'm outside
Had I done what she said,
The child would be dead
Midnight Blue throws more charges
'Til his dad interrupts his barges
His dad said can't you tell your sister is telling a lie
You don't make a good woman like your wife cry
You're still a boy
Who thinks women are toys
Hang up my phone
Don't you yell at her no more
I hang up first

Need to leave here before I burst
Fell asleep with the pot on
Wake up house full of smoke
I'm 'bout to choke
Call my own dad
No questions asked, he's on the way glad
A twenty-five minute drive takes my dad ten
I'm packed, baby dressed, and ready then
Back to the house of hate
He and Grandmother grab my child like bait
Mother is still the same
With my child a new game
When I get back to work
Get a phone message that makes me go berserk
Wench had the nerve to call my job
She threatens to rob me of my child
Wench says she and her brother had made plans
To take my child from me
Midnight Blue signed over his rights to her
By the time I get back home
My child will be gone
Tell my boss what's up
He says go come back when you can
'Cause your husband isn't a man
Get the tape of the message from human resources
See my mother from around the corner
She says calm down you're not a goner
Take the tape to court
Give the tape and a full report
I wish you could stay here with me
But I've got no room you see

I tell Dad who gets mad

That makes me sad
I'll make some calls **he says**
We leave my real mother out of the loop
'Cause she still wants me out to boot
Don't care where she goes **she shouts**
I just want her out

I go back to the other house to pack
The Aunt's child runs down screaming come quick
My mother is sick
I run up the stairs
It's the *wench*
This is what she wails
Wench screams my husband and my brother says I shouldn't kick your
tail
I told her I'm ready just touch me so I
Can knock you out your shoes
For I have nothing left to lose

Wench screams, "What on Earth have I done to you?"
(Is she for real, when it's my *child* she tried to steal)
I say, I've got a list I can check twice
For you've never been nice
If that's all you've got to say
I got things to do—so go away

Wench again wails
I should kick your tail

I say I've got nothing left to lose, I can surely promise you I'll knock
you out your shoes
If that is all you got to say
I've got things to do

Can you for once shut up too

In the background, the aunts pull back the table as I walk out the door
I don't want to hear no more
Halfway down the stairs

Wench yells some more
I'm gonna pray for you!

I say, "Oh no, pray for yourself and **Midnight Blue!**"
Wench ain't worth her underwear
For me to go to jail
Had she touched me, I would have claimed self-defense and got off
That ***wench*** was just barely worth my breath I scoff

ANOTHER NEW WORLD

Dad had made his calls to his relatives is where I'm to go
It doesn't feel right to me you know
I had to give up my good job
They were paying for my college with a nod
All I needed was enough support with some time
I'd found another apartment further up state to call mine
It would have been a longer train ride in
But mother wants me out right then
I haven't really learned enough of the world's language
To be able to manage
Now I'm in a new world

I know from the moment my feet hit the tarmac
This wasn't for me, and my child
Don't get this place, it's another world
The language here I don't know
Makes living a hard way to go
Things here are hidden
They smile at you and their words are bitter

It took four months to get a job
At my relatives' I feel something wrong
I was right when my dad showed up with a sad song
I'm doing the best I can
Then it dawns on me I'm in another frying pan
They don't really want me here
They really don't care
It's because of my dad
If I do something wrong they can make him mad
Then he'll come here fast as he can
I'm sorry I won't be used

By being falsely accused
Then **my cousin** does this rant
We were told you were a whore
Running from a pimp who's a chore
You weren't supposed to succeed
You had no skills
Just the ability to give men thrills
You're not really wanted here
You've got too many problems for us to care

I tune her out like white noise
Never once did I lose my poise
I start making plans to leave
It's not the frying pan, but the fire I'm in I believe

LAST CHANCE

Moved out, got my own
They are surprised pretend to groan
Working every day at a white collar job
Got a car to get to and from work with a nod
Finding babysitters isn't easy
Leaving my child makes me queasy
In the meantime, **Midnight Blue** begs for another chance
People calling saying he's learned his lesson now
He'll do better some how
Your child needs a dad
Put away your mad
(If I do this, it's not for love)
You don't want to anger GOD above

Throwing the Bible in my face,
I've got no choice 'cause I have my own place
Okay one last chance
This has nothing to do with love or romance
Led to believe my child needs his dad
It doesn't take thirty days for me to get mad
Nothing has changed
Just a different place that's strange
The same thing **Midnight Blue** did when he was with his own dad
He does with me making me mad
Midnight Blue halfheartedly looks for work
Claims he needs my car to do it, *the jerk*
Claims the Child needs to be with a sitter full time
Midnight Blue doesn't look for a job, 'cause I've got mine
Play around most of the day
A sitter I still have to pay
Doesn't pick me up from work on time

Doesn't pick up the Child, tell me, he's mine
I insist on getting my tubes tied
Midnight Blue asks why
I don't want any more of your seed
To turn into more children we don't need
Midnight Blue says that not it
You want to sleep with more men, think I won't find out so you won't
get hit
I reply that's not true
It's either you go snip-snip, or I do

The truth he doesn't need to know, 'cause he never attended one doc-
tor's appointment to hear what was said
The next pregnancy I have, I will surely be dead
I get my tubes tied and sighed
Midnight Blue mad calls his mother and ***wench*** sister pretends to cry
Now she will cheat on me for sure
She doesn't want to take care of me the way you said she should

Then **Midnight Blue** breaks my car
Doesn't tell I'm stuck at work too far
Get a call from the babysitter too
My child hasn't been picked up either and she's blue
Find someone left at work to get me and my child home
Midnight Blue is sitting there acting like nothing's wrong
What happened—I ask strong
Midnight Blue: Car's broke and I didn't know what to do,
So I did nothing, the rest is up to you

I walk seven miles or more to the nearest store
Getting a battery, hoping the car will start
Get picked up by a stranger who says my walking isn't smart
Back at the house, the dinner I left out wasn't even fixed

Midnight Blue: Not my job I'm starving, he's miffed
The ultimate—my child in dirty diapers chewing on a cracker
Lord help me please, 'cause **Midnight Blue** I'm gonna smack him
Change the diaper and get my child some food
Ignoring **Midnight Blue** I fix my own
Get into a bath 'cause my feet are sore

No **Midnight Blue** doesn't think I'm gonna give him some
Don't touch me I say, you get none

Take him somewhere and get him a job
Midnight Blue complains says the money isn't enough for a nod
The last straw, a park movie for my child
Midnight Blue on the phone to his mother complaining all the while
Midnight Blue: Mother says you can't do anything right
He slaps me while I'm driving, and I can't fight
Turning the car, doing ninety-miles an hour and heading for the nearest
wall,
I'm gonna kill him finally after all

Midnight Blue swallows and says real calm
You forgot the backseat has your child

Slamming on brakes, doing a 360 degree turn
I go back across three lanes, through oncoming traffic, my temper on
burn

Your mother, or me—you have your choice
Midnight Blue: You won't take care of me—my mother
I say: Tell your mother to send you a ticket
One-way back to where you came
'Cause life with you is insane
That's it, I've had enough

When we get home, pack your stuff

Next day when I drop him at the airport
Midnight Blue: when did you stop loving me
I never did, you never listened came my retort
Speeding off I leave him at the curb happy as can be

DIVORCE

When I get to my lawyer's, he's beet red
"What's wrong with you?" I said
Lawyer: You married a fool
Who thinks he could use you as a tool
Me: Oh Lord, here we go
Do I really want to know—
Lawyer: He wants child support dropped from 900 dollars a month to
300 a month
Says you make more than him, and can get good jobs
Wants alimony like I'll let him rob
He also wants you to pay for his transportation, room, and board
For when he visits, is he out of his gourd
Either that or bounce the kid on a plane
Is he really insane—
Where was your father before all of this
He should have killed him before he got close to you
It's not right for him to give you the blues
I'm not giving in to his demands
This divorce is definitely my command
Me: simply it's this
I want to be back to *Miss*
I'll take the 300 dollars a month if it sets me free
I want my name back so I can be *me*
Lawyer: 300 dollars won't cover diapers and food
Clothes or shelter too
Are you sure those are the only two things you want
'Cause I got something for his taunts
Me: Here are the copies of the restraining orders I've got against him,
his **wench** sister and crazy mother
I just want to make sure I will not be bothered
Lawyer: Oh, don't worry I'll work it out that way

He really has no say
Friend of the court will get the money and give it to you
I'll let them know domestic violence is an issue
So he will get supervised visits too
I doubt that he will take the time
To make the arrangements, which will be fine
Then you can throw him in jail where he belongs
'Cause he's a boy, not a man, which is so wrong

I go to court and get it signed
I'm really free this time

IN A HOLE

Thanks to Midnight Blue, before he left new apartment was signed
Can't get out of it in a bind
My child gets his own room
Running around he goes *ZOOM*!
He makes a friend with the boy down the hall
I meet Navy Blue first, then the mother who says the kids have a ball
My child has an outlet they take him fishing
He comes home grinning with the boy's dad
I say, Sweetheart I'm glad
Navy Blue says hey why don't you come down for a movie
My wife and I and the kids, it'll be groovy
With my child looking up at me
I say okay this one time we'll see
Dinner is hot and ready
Send Navy Blue back to his place steady
At first, things seem to be okay
Then things take a sudden turn one day

NAVY BLUE

Woke up in the night feeling bright
Did I forget to turn out the light?

Rolled over in the bed
Navy Blue face greets me instead

What the hell you doing here
As I look at him suddenly feeling much fear

Navy Blue: Left my wife in bed 'cause I'd rather screw you instead
Me: Return to your wife, she really needs you
Navy Blue: No she don't, she just makes me blue

With that said, he slams in me
I lay there like a tree
Scheming to give him the knee

Navy Blue: Don't you dare
I'd kill your child and make you wish you were dead
With thoughts of my child in the next room in his bed
I dared not move instead

Navy Blue: Oh, you're one of them who'll work the hell out of me
I don't answer—I become a dead tree
Finally finished, he rolls to the left
As the blood flows out me wet

Tired and spent, I think he's asleep
I try to slide out of the bed neat
Navy Blue: Where you going you don't have to sneak in your own
house

Me: Got to go to the bathroom, thought you were asleep, and wanted
to be quiet as a mouse
Navy Blue: Well go then and take your time

I ease out of the bedroom grab my child and move faster than this
rhyme
Run outta my house
Faster than a scared mouse
Grabbing a knife with a free hand as I pass
Hoping like hell the car has some gas

About a week and a police report too
The wife calls out of the blue
Did my husband hurt you?

Your husband raped me I said
She says here's what **Navy Blue** told me instead
You were mistress number fifty-two
'Cause **Navy Blue** watched you and knew your every move too
On the day we borrowed your car and house keys
Navy Blue asked me to copy them please
I really thought you knew
I had no idea he would rape you

CHANGES

Ever since the rape things at work aren't going real well
The chatter about me has increased I can tell
I can't get the hang of this is there something I missed
Trying hard to be a loner
Work, my child, and home
No place or time for me to roam
Crock pot dinners, homemade biscuits, and corn bread on the side
Lay away my child's clothes, putting the old ones aside
Doing all I can isn't enough
My mind filled with so much stuff
My ex's family with the help of my mother
Harass my dad's family here
Nobody seems to care
My child is important to me
So is being free
Since the rape, I've been forced to move
That didn't go smooth
Had to break my lease
Find a different place no feelings to release
Thought if I found one close to my job
Things would be better somehow
Exhausted physically and mentally
No friends to talk to, I can't trust anyone to let them get close
Nowhere else to go when I need it most
Trying to keep my child happy
We go the playground on sunny days
Then dinner and home we stay
Away on vacation so my child can see the world
Trying to let my child be the child I could never be
No men for me

Get falsely accused of child abuse
Everyone allowing themselves to be well-used
As tools to get my child from me
Not gonna happen this is deliberate, because I want to stay free
Midnight Blue doesn't make the arrangements for supervised visits
And he doesn't pay child support
But he keeps making these false, unfounded reports
The harassment is wearing on me
I'm tired. Can't relax, changes come with being free

ONYX

I come home from work and what do I see
Some strange man looking at me
Looking after my child, big as can be

What happened to my babysitter I said
Onyx: Oh she left me here instead
Okay I'm here now I say
Onyx: Oh no, it isn't going to work that way

As things progressed, and I couldn't get him out
I found out how this came about

It seems the landlord who lived downstairs
Had been coming up short in his drug shares

Thinking how he could come up with the extra money quick,
He sent the drug dealer to me in hopes he could give me a lick
The plan to turn me out real slick

Landlord: I'm sure she would do 'cause no man has done her in a
year or two
She's simply not very smart
It shouldn't matter what happens to her heart
She should be easy to turn out
For no man has come about

But the truth about me
Very difficult to see
Either I'll toss you out or get out
I'm not about to lose my free

I managed to flip the script
And get out with as much as I could grip

Onyx couldn't understand why he set me free
And all **Onyx** got was the TV

ANOTHER MOVE

I had no choice but to quit my job,
Things didn't work out I'd been fired with a nod
I really hate this state
Can't go back to my own too late
Dad takes my child
I hope that's mild
Get the letter from a school in another city that is approved
I'm gonna move

Get there, it's not gonna work
It's too expensive, the prices give me a jerk
Next step try to get a job
Mother calls and complains with a nod
Dad and Grandmother and my child are having too good of a time
She demands he returns to be mine
Telling her I'm not ready for him doesn't matter
Moving too quickly, my mind shatters

I did the best I could
Didn't know I moved into the hood
Poor thing my child comes back
Working hard, but everything is under attack
Working part-time I thought the state would pay
For my child to go to daycare that's what they say
That doesn't happen of course
State: You can make 10 plus dollars an hour
So therefore, we have no power

Then my child gets sick
Gotta find somebody quick
Things continue to fall apart

I'm tired can't think
So much for a new start
If only my dad and grandmother could keep him one more year
Everything would be straight and clear
My child would be in school
So I can work and go to school part-time too
Then things would be cool

Dad wants to agree
He really wants to help me
Things continue to fall apart
Mother complains from the start

I'm tired, sick, and looking for another job
Mother's threats mess with my heart
Mother: If you don't come get this child
I'll tell his father you abused him and went wild

To make sure her threats are a promise meant to be
My ex's attack my dad sure as can be
Terrorizing my child, I get the call
Not sure who this man is that's in my house—
Last thing I remember was dinner, and then the hospital
Blood pressure 50/50 and I walked in
The paramedics said don't bother her with a grin
Laying on the gurney, I respond your blood pressure machine is broke
The male nurse looks at me afraid to tell me the truth 'cause I might go
into a stroke

Now I don't know what day it is
My child on the phone is this a quiz
Ask my child if he's okay
My child: Bad things happened yesterday

I ask if he met his dad
That makes him mad
My Child: That can't be my dad he talks bad about my mom
Me: Okay what did he say
My Child: They threatened Grandpa, said they was going to take me
Grandpa say over his dead body and I hid behind his knee
But Mom, I took the gifts they gave me
Me: Hold tight my precious child
Momma's gonna come get you somehow
Mother snatches the phone, gets back on the line
I'll send the ticket by nine

I tell this man I gotta go
Sick, tired, not sure what has happened to me
My vision blurs just barely able to see
Now I'm really stuck
Feel like I been hit by a truck
Had no choice, but to get my child
Things are a mess but we'll make it somehow

INTERLUDE OR INTERMISSION

BEFORE THIS OUR ROUTINE

5:00 to 5:59 am get ready for work, put meat in crock-pot,
and make lunch
5:59 to 6:00 am *THUD*! Five, four, three, *THAWCK*!
Good morning son
Morning Mom
6:00 to 7:00 am breakfast of oatmeal or Cream of Wheat,
and get child ready
Walk the seven miles to daycare, my child and me, singing as we go
7:30 to 9:00 am bus to work
9:00 am to 5 pm work and pick up child from daycare
5 pm to 6pm make our way home, stop at park on sunny days
6 pm to 7:30 pm dinner on the table get child ready for bed
7:30 pm Child in his room plenty for him to do
I get dishes done, and work on hair for next day
When he gets quiet, I go in his room to make sure he's in his bed
Sometimes he's in a ball on the floor
Make sure he's tucked in bed
By 11 pm I'm in the bed
Saturday is breakfast out and cleaning house
Sunday is church, and Wednesday night is church

OUT OF THE MOUTH OF BABES

My mom has big hair
She has two extra pillows for my head to spare

I need two, one for me and one for my mom

My mom looks good everyday
I'm going to my room 'cause when my mom gets mad, she'll make
you pay

Little Thug: I got hundred dollar shoes
My Child: I ate smothered chicken and rice with biscuits what you eat
Little Heifer: McDonalds, his mom can't cook

Mom will I grow as big as Grandpa
Mom: I don't know how tall you will get dear
No Mom, I mean down here

Anyone who talks bad about my mom is not my family!

You like my mom 'cause she needs a husband and I need a dad

Continued

JET BLACK

Dear Lord how could this be
My only child is dead 'cause of me

I didn't want a lot
Just a good man to fill the family spot

Why did this happen to me
What was it I could not see

To make sure to get under my skin
Jet Black drugged me to live in sin

Then I get sick
Couldn't see this evil pick

So tired, mind blown
I sleep for three weeks
My body worn and weak
Jet Black woke me to bathe and eat
Made it look like he was taking care of me

While in a haze, he royally screwed me
Then my child came back
Within six months *Jet Black* attacked
Busted my baby's head wide open

I'm at work, not joking
Get an emergency call
That my child took a nasty fall
Took a cab to the hospital as fast as I could

Couldn't understand what was up at the hospital
Everyone looking at me funny
Jet Black looked at me and called me honey

By the time I was allowed to get to my son's hospital bed
I could see he was already dead

Docs: Why didn't you call
When he first took that fall?
I was told he was awake and fine
I didn't know, *Jet Black* had handed me a line

The next morning the cops took us in
Then proceeded to tell me about *Jet Black's* evil sin

No!!!
Jet Black couldn't have killed my only child
I know I was sick, my mind gone wild
My sweet innocent loving child
The only one in the world who loved me
No way!!
Jet Black killed him how could this be

Lost in a state of shock
Put everything in hock
Got cursed out, spit on, and slapped
Like any of that will bring my child back

No one believed, I didn't know
Everyone chose instead to believe I put on a show
For once in my life I could not get away
Fast enough to protect my own child, I put him in harm's way

When all I really wanted was a good friend
Someone on whom I could depend

It was just me and my child
No one for me to talk to, our life was mild

I was tired, sick, lonely, and blue
Jet Black claimed that he was true
If I'd only knew
I'd move again, and flew

He was my only child
His momma was never wild
Trying to fulfill everyone else's dream
Caused my child and my life to be very hard and mean

Maybe if I had stuck to my own pace
My child would still be here to run the race
Doctor's didn't know if or how they would deliver
All the talk made my heart quiver

For I wasn't supposed to be pregnant, you see
There really wasn't any room inside of me

I prayed Lord about this death date
If He could reassign another fate
If it's for me to die
Let me live long enough to see his eyes
If death is his fate
Can we reassign the date?

For I want a longer time for me and my boy
Long enough for me and him to enjoy,

God answered my prayer and death stayed
I didn't realize it was only delayed

Everybody created hell and strife
Making for a miserable life
You'd never believe a year before he was born
I was his father's wife

His father's people with my mothers help planned you see
To drive me crazy and take my child from me

My mother's anger, resentment, and bitterness cast
Came from a long past

Scared and running to avoid all kinds of crazy schemes
Caused my child and my life to be very hard and mean

Maybe if I had taken a stand and went at my own pace
My child would still be here to run the race
Holding onto my child tight, with all my might
I didn't realize a stranger would take up the same plight

Leaving for work my child was alive
By nightfall no one could revive

Emotional and physically exhausted and broke,
I didn't realize I had suffered a mental stroke

Needing all the help I can,
I turned to a stranger who was a devil of a man

The night my child died
I was in too much shock to cry

It wasn't until I was at the police station
I found out about *Jet Black's* devil nation

I was told my child fell down the stairs
Found out *Jet Black's* lies came in pairs

I was told it was an accident, he couldn't stop
The truth was a blunt instrument *Jet Black* beat my child across the
top

Jet Black beat my child like another grown man
Killed him, and lied the best he can

The child who was supposed to die at birth
Gave me five years of joy and mirth

The death that I thought was stayed
Was only delayed

What if I hadn't gone to work that day?
Would death have gone away?

Knowing I could never have another
I was proud of being that child's mother

FUNERAL

In shock I still can't believe
How well I had been deceived
Mother has arrived—I'm locked in hell
No comfort verbal rocks of all kinds
Whatever comes to her mind,
Where is the ending bell
Mother: You are no longer a mother, 'cause you allowed your child to
die
Looking at Mother, I strangle my cry
Mother: You're worthless—this is all your fault
Blow after blow without letting up, I'm distraught
My lungs ache I can no longer breathe
Then I start to wheeze
Dad come back just as I grab my inhaler
He missed Mother's last blows
Watching me, he's in pain he tries not to show
Me: I wasn't there, I was at work when everything went down
Thought things would be better in this town
The crazy ex's show up too
Funny how they couldn't arrange the supervised visits, but make it to
the funeral
Ex's: We are here to prove she's the one who abused and killed this
child

'Cause the child was signed over to me by my brother, the **wench**
sister says
I just turn to solid rock
Ex's: The police told us to come get our proof
I'm wondering if I'm in a spoof

Don't know how much more I can take

No peace for me to bury my only child
Preacher gets mad slams the casket shut
Preacher: If this child was abused, the Mother came first you nut

Finally, this mess ends
My other mom and my dad try to protect me as I bend
Crazy **wench** of an ex-sister-in-law has the nerve to try to reach me
first
Wench sister-in-law: Is there anything you need
My fists balled in my pocket, 'bout to burst
My dad jumps between us first
Dad: She don't need nothing from any of you
Why don't you go away and take him too

In a huff, she grabs her brother
Wench: Come on, we need to get to the police station and blow this
chick's cover

Get my child's body to the cemetery
I want to scream enough already
My other mom loses it and starts to moan
Please don't leave her here alone
Of course, my mother pays her no attention
She makes Dad leave without hesitation
Now I'm alone, left to deal with this fate
All of this, because of a bad summer date

MORE LIES

In less than a week, there are more lies
Why is that not a big surprise
Dad gets royally pissed, and calls me direct
Send me the file you got I know you're a wreck
I don't see how they could tell such bold face lies
When there is a warrant for my ex's arrest, the **wench** and his mother
have restraining orders against them, so their arrest too
No way they got that information from the police station
'Cause they would have gotten arrested in a split second
I send dad the entire file with all the papers from friend of the court
The truth in a black in white report
Including the divorce decree
So he can see what I had to do, to get free
I don't know what he did with it, but it worked
Not one more lie was spoken out of turn
For that matter everyone suddenly disappears
Funny how that happens when the truth reveals you're in arrears
Nothing left for me to do, the trial is about to start
What am I to do with my shattered heart?

TRIAL DAY 1

What's this I can't believe—
The ultimate plan to deceive
In court that first day
I find out **Jet Black's** name ain't his name—no way
Pay stubs *FAKE*
IRS tax forms last ten years, *FAKE*
Supervisor from the job *FAKE*
Nothing 'bout this man that he told me was real
No. No, it got worse
I can't even curse
This was a contract hit
Set by my ex and his crew
It's been five years—I never knew
The hit was for *me*
But he took my child out instead
This revelation is too much for my head
Even without evidence or proof,
My gut says it's true
Forced to deal with the revelations by myself,
This can't be happening—no way
I feel like I'm watching from a shelf
So ends the first day of trial
I'm in a daze this is unbelievable somehow

VENDETTA

Five-year vendetta turned contract hit
You and your family told so many lies
If the people who listened wanted the truth
For a fee, they could have gotten it in black and white
You didn't want me out of your sight

Five-year vendetta turned contract hit
My friends, my dad, and I gave you so many chances to leave me
I tried to send you on dates, you wouldn't go—
Every time you gave some cock-a-nanny excuse to not do right
I told you it was fine by me if you left my sight

Five-year vendetta turned contract hit
Did you even bother to tell how you and your **wench** sister had come
up with this crazy plan
To drive me crazy, and take my child from me best you can
So this way I wouldn't have a choice, but to stay stuck with you
You knew there was no way I was gonna leave, and risk not being able
to see my own child too

Five-year vendetta turned contract hit
No wonder you had so much false information
You claimed came from a police station
But your plan backfired on you
Your hit man killed my child, left me alive and blue

Five-year vendetta turned contract hit
You forget to tell how you left me with a two-week-old child
Thinking your sister would snatch him before you came back
That was the reason I left after that attack

Five-year vendetta turned contract hit
What about the fact that you handed me three hundred dollars for an
abortion
When that didn't happen, you did everything to make me miscarry
That your **wench** sister jumped in my face, and said she wanted to kick
my tail
I told her I ain't got time for someone not worth their underwear
I can't even tell my dad
No way—I'm sending Dad to jail 'cause he got mad

Five-year vendetta turned contract hit
You took two lives from me
When all I wanted was to be free
I never wanted to stay alive
It was, and still is, GOD's decision that I stay alive

TRIAL DAY 2

Here we go, another day of new revelations
Discovering this man was hired by my ex to take me out
Had me mad enough to scream and shout
Now it's the second day
I've been asked to leave the courtroom—**NO WAY**
Prosecution: Ma'am you're here by yourself
We are going over the autopsy notes, not something on a shelf
You won't be able to handle what was done to your child
What this man did ain't pretty, to put it mild

So here in the hallway I sit,
I feel like I've lost all my wits
My eyes fill with tears
I've aged beyond my years
I don't notice that my tears turn into wails
Like they would flood the hallway needing pails
When I blink, the detective is looking at me
I think it's him, my tears make it hard to see
Upset and angry 'bout all the noise
Detective: I sure hope this is for your child, not that person in there
calling himself a man
'Cause he's no good, the absolute worse person, damn
Me: I'm crying for my child; did all I could, I assure you sir, I never
was wild
Detective: Go home, you're no good here, you won't last—wait 'til
this day has passed

Getting up disorientated, and nauseated too
I forget to eat
Feeling the heat
Somehow, I make it to the place I call home
All I can do is crawl in my bed and moan

HERE WE GO

Got a call from a friend of mine
Sounds like her youngest baby daddy reached the end of his time
My Friend: I need you

I don't want to go, try to tell her she got nothing to gain
Especially since he has remarried
The torch for him she carried
My Friend: Got to do this
Okay, okay the next thing moving I won't miss
Pick up two new outfits one for me and one for her daughter
To say I'm on the next thing smoking is putting it mild
Doing what I can do to fulfill my part,
Not much you can do with a shattered heart
It's been three months since my child died,
Two days of trial, all I do is cry
No one is there for me
Mother's Day is coming—don't know how to be
Can't keep my mind on track
Looking at my girlfriend in her sorrow, my brain cracks
Next thing I know **Ebony Black** is in my face
Don't remember seeing him in this place
Try as I might, I can't shake him
Stuck in a car, he jumps in on a whim

Funeral and wake over—I run home
Now **Ebony Black** is ringing my phone
How you get my number? I try not to shout
Your girl gave it to me, **Ebony Black** says as I pout
We live miles away
Don't worry **Ebony Black** says, I have someplace to stay
Hanging up the phone
All I can do is moan

The cemetery has banned me
'Cause when I get there, I cry and wail like a banshee
They say: Don't come back 'til you can stand on your feet
Not drop to the floor, pounding your fists
Getting up isn't neat

Ebony Black through my girl is loud, brash, rude, and ghetto as hell
Every time **Ebony Black** around, I look for a bell
Saying he's a preacher, **Ebony Black** makes friends with my pastor at church
The associates all smirk
What can I do? I don't want to attend another day of trial alone
If only **Ebony Black** can keep his mouth shut, I groan
Needing to prove a point
I don't want the killer of my child thinking he can come back after he's done with the joint
So I take **Ebony Black** calling himself a *preacher* to court

Hoping to get my point across,
All of a sudden, **Ebony Black** steps to the judge like he's the boss
Great, how do I get out of this
It's my dad that I miss—
At the family reunion **Ebony Black** comes up to me with Uncle and Dad
Looking at me, **Ebony Black says**: it's okay to marry
I do my best not to get mad,
I understand poor Dad don't know what to do,
He can't handle his and my shades of black and blue
When **Ebony Black** and I get a moment alone,
I ask what would he have done if my dad said *no*
Ebony Black: We'll just have to live together in sin
'Cause I'm not letting you go
Swallowing hard—payment for emotional services rendered is marriage
I'm stuck again

EBONY BLACK

If I only knew how to peg
I'd known my husband was jackleg

Took advantage of a tragic grief situation,
Acted like he knew the right prescription

Left alone inside my desperate grief
He came into my life claiming he'll provide relief

Helped me make it through the murder trial
As each time I did wail

Preacher Ebony Black missed the last day when the verdict came in
Five years' probation, and a year in the mental ward for my child
killer's sin
Judge was mad 'cause there was no proof that I helped this come about
I was at work! I shout

Alone and steeped in much grief,
He called himself, providing relieve

Didn't touch me or do a thing
Until I had that wedding ring

Then within six months, everything came to a front
When on me he jumped—the runt

First, he jumped on my back
I said, "You need to do better than that—"

Seven hours we physically fought,

All my grief, pain, anger, and naught
Came out during that attack
For I fought back

If I had been home when my child was killed,
There would have been at least three deaths more still
All that came out of me
As I fought my husband, I couldn't see

Just before I could escape
He did try to rape
Escape from him I did
At the landlady I hid

Then in the security TV
Here come cops two, maybe three

My husband claimed I was missing three days
No officer, it didn't turn out that way

He jumped on my back
And started an attack

The officer laughing real hard
Said you are messed up—but you tore him up like a card

What do you want us to do
Get one of us out of here, 'cause I'm black and blue

Cops took him away,
In my depressed state, I whipped him that day

SCREAM

From the time of my birth
I've caught hell on this earth
Forced to believe
There was no love for me to receive
It's been proven to be true
For I wear shades of black and blue
Nothing but bad invaded my life
Crazy men chased me screaming, *"Be my wife!"*
No peace, no free
I can't find me
Wounds and gashes are open sores
Shattered heart can't take no more
Shame and blame are my chains
Always in pain
My chains are tightly wound
'Cause I'm naked as I'm bound,
The weight of life is on my shoulders
Like large oversized boulders
There's no one I can trust
My chains break as they rust
Cutting open more sores
Ice fills the voids, deficits, and pores
No longer care what's in store
The darkness of life engulfs me,
I can no longer see
My mouth opens wide
And...

I...

...SCREAM

THE WHEAT

Matthew 13:24-30
Separating the Wheat from the Tares
And the Burdens that are left to bare

WHERE WERE YOU LORD

Where were you LORD before you found me
And took me back

Where were you LORD before that sea
Over took me

Where were you LORD before your genuine
Love took flight

Where were you LORD before you and I
Became real tight

Where were you LORD before I became alive

Where were you LORD before you said
My daughter, arise

Where were you LORD during the time of
All that pain

Where were you LORD while you
Made me tame

Where were you LORD
During that attack

Where were you LORD when
You set me free

THE LORD SAID HERE I AM

The LORD said here I am
Whether or not you are in a jam

The LORD said here I am
Come to me just as you are
For I am not that far

The LORD said here I am
Waiting patiently to set you free
I am waiting for you to just be

The LORD said here I am
Waiting for you to stop the fight
If you let me take over we'll be real tight

The LORD said here I am
Let me flow
I'll give you that spiritual glow

The LORD said here I am
I did not move
You were in the wrong groove

The LORD said HERE AM I

COUNSELING

For the first time since high school in my life
I'm in counseling to resolve the strife

My counselor said
I can't believe with all the issues you and your husband have
Neither of you did the math
You shouldn't have gotten married
Not with all the pain you're both carrying
It's obvious he took advantage of you 'cause you're alone
Your family doesn't care two cents, and probably caused you to moan
Before we can get to the issues of today
We have to go back to yesterday
Like the layers of an onion, we have to peel back one layer at a time
So we can resolve each and every crime
Your wounds aren't fresh—they're infected
instead of behaving like the utmost rejected
You will be in counseling back and forth most of your life
If you do the work, counseling will lessen the strife
As you allow GOD to mend your wounds
Your testimony and strength will help women all the way to the moon
Right now, we need to move you from denial to reality
So we can start with why you're so angry

I said:
Couldn't figure out how to get rid of him
Couldn't figure out how to get away from all the bad men
Always I have a plan on what I need to do
Always some man tells me some Bible verse that says I'm wrong
Without me in their life, they can't be strong
Especially when they see all I have
I work, pay my own bills,

had no debt 'til they came along,
have my own place, nobody takes care of me—but me
Hard as I try, I can't stay free
Tired of all the black and blue
Tell me can counseling really help me

Counselor said
If you do the work, with the help of GOD you will be free

MOTHER'S DAY

Open my eyes LORD why am I still here
Mother's Day was never celebrated for me, nobody cared
Fighting with the mantra and broken record in my head
You're no longer a mother 'cause you allowed your child to be dead
This is what my mother said

Sitting in church, all I do is cry
As the preacher asks all mothers stand, flowers coming by
Suddenly two women grab me on either side,
Pull me to my feet, so I stand—when all I want to do is hide
Whispering in my ear: You're still a mother, it's okay to cry
All I feel is faint, and want to die

They become my sisters to help me through
They comforted me in my shades of black and blue
Even though I'm frozen, they become more than my friend
Chipping at the ice to try to help me to mend
LORD GOD is still watching over me,
For HE sent me a few sisters who are real and true as can be

CHILDREN

Sitting in church, one of the young ladies comes running,
dropping her baby in my lap
She said, "I'll be right back,"
I remember those days when there was no one for me
Struggling with my baby, and I had to pee

Another church event felt a familiar *THUD*
Looking down at my leg,
a toddler staring up at me like, "What's up Bud?"
Hoisting the child into the air,
A mom screams with care
He got away from me through the crowd,
Tried to call him but it was too loud

Watched a mom at the door of daycare say good-bye
To her child with tears in her eye
I remember dropping to my knees on the floor,
My head pressed against my child's,
staring into his eyes saying, "I love you,"
My child responds, "Mom, I love you more,"

Since his death, GOD sends me children to remind me of his birth
All the things we did that brought me mirth
Even though life was tough and sad,
We did the best with what we had

GOING THROUGH THE MOTIONS

Hanging on to GOD real tight
Doing my best to stay out of sight
Going through the motions of work, church, and home
At night, to GOD I moan
GOD sent me a sister who I could talk to 'bout anything
Helping her, and being with her takes my mind off things
Keeping busy in ministry helps me forget about the wounds and chains
I don't think about the pain
A couple of good men try to call
All I can think about are the ones who deliberately made me fall
I don't like doing anything I can't figure out or do well
I'm not ready for men—can't you tell
Perfecting my disappearing acts,
Ready for battle I'm first to attack
Cut all ties to family and old friends
Gotta figure out who caused me the most trouble
so contact can permanently end
The fakers, takers, and breakers who caused so much strife
When all I wanted was a free life
Just as GOD and I starting getting tight
The Church splits overnight
struggling to hold on 'cause the Senior Pastor has been a real friend
GOD says your membership here has to end

RUNNING

Changing jobs, can't handle the stress
This job has too much mess
Get a job with my dream company
Let go of two men chasing me
A third hanging on for dear life
But he has so much strife
Finally, he comes to me with a scenario so like my own
Oh no your wife is gonna get your child killed I moan
Just knowing it's 'cause of me
I plan to disappear so he can be free

LORD GOD, let me run this last time
You need to hide me from men who scream, "*Mine!*"
They seem to always find my key
Here LORD, keep it hidden safe as can be

The LORD said
All right, I'll do this—keep and hide your keys
'Cause next time you're stuck,
unless the man takes them from me

At the same time, two women from work
Who have befriended me in spite of my quirks
One tells me 'bout her church
The other another place across town

Grabbing both opportunities
Change church and pack my stuff in storage
A glitch comes up out of nowhere
My friend with the new place says it's too torn down to move in there
You can stay with me and my husband for a while

Save what you can, then move with style

I move in with her
and at the new church I jump into ministries
Too busy for counseling or to think

A pager on one hip, cell phone on the other,
and keys to company cars
Think I've got things beat this far
GOD starts chipping at the ice
One woman at church makes nice

Living with my friend and her husband, I get scared
Remembering the man whose wife helped him rape me—I become
unfair
Need to run again,
Woman at church says I have a place, no one there
Without thinking moving again from here

PARTNERS

In one ministry, I have a partner who stands six-feet-nine
He's like a friend, bodyguard—and he's not screaming, "*Mine*!"
Instead, he just walks by my side
Working together in ministry, he deals with the men
I concentrate on the women
He's a GOD-send

No worries 'bout men chasing me,
He deflects them, corrects them, keeps me safe and free
We work so well together the married women *ooh* and *ahh*
You two will marry after a while,
He and I look at each other and say, "*NO Way chile*,"

Being so busy, I get sick
Married women run get him quick
This is how you care for her when she gets like this
Half-conscious, can't breathe
or talk, in my head I'm screaming, "I'm not his miss!"

Rushed to the hospital, I'm in there four days
Pneumonia, fluid around the heart, and a half-collapsed lung
The woman with house, whose ministry I carry, has news to be sprung

ANOTHER WENCH

As I lay upon my hospital bed,
Wench says her son wants the house I'm in instead
But she'll give me some time
Three months to find somewhere to be mine
All I could do is blink
Mind went into think
Three months—my job would have given me a promotion and a raise
Six months I'd have a new car,
and my own house with the money I saved
Her house wasn't worth a dime
Tore up from the floor to the ceiling,
there was only one room for me to live in
The bathroom so filthy all I can do is wipe and swipe
Go to work early just to get a shower
Why the worst ones think they have power
Feeling devalued, and running due to fear
I took her house, 'cause I didn't care
Now got to change my plans
Sick and busy doesn't allow for that

LINKS ADDED

Her lies spread through the church
Don't know what she said, I'm in a lurch
Life must still go on
I'm trying to keep my department at work together
Which means I'm the one gotta be strong
They can't know there's something wrong

A woman with six kids needs food
Wench's family at the hospital,
waiting for their mother to die soon
Ministry work still needs me
What time do I have free
Her sister-in-law has a special event,
I'm helping the sister-in-law with that
know better than to vent

Can't say a thing
Accused of wanting her bling
Can't take no more, had enough,
Still sick telling docs I'm at home—as a bluff
Truth is I'm back to work, gotta be tough

Leave the country with all my pain meds,
Holed up in a hotel room, hoping for death
All I do is watch TV, and sleep
Body is so tired and weak
When I finally return,
Church calls a meeting with me alone
All I can do is groan
The words *we love you* fall like stones on glass,
I'm the one accused of behaving like an ass

More links added to my chains of shame and blame
Boulders added the same
No one wants to hear the truth
Yes, it's always my fault
After all, it's what I was taught

My wounds open and bleed
Growth from the seeds

Not sure what my ministry partner knows
Isn't that how it goes
Instead of free, I'd hoped for stability
That's what I thought GOD had for me

UNFAIR

LORD, why is life so unfair
The ones who don't make the effort or care
Are the ones who get away with everything—no price do they pay,
But people like me, who try so hard and work our fingers to the bone
Are the ones left to pay the price and groan,
As many times as I've moved
To get away from people disturbing my groove
There is no way I'd want that wench's house
Especially since it wasn't fit for a mouse
Why did she find it necessary to lie
'Cause I didn't respond or cry
LORD I've been too busy to think
About what to do with what she said in a blink

I'm still so sick
My brain never did function right to be quick
Not in my personal life, the job is different
They have access to all the tools needed
and therefore not equivalent

Six months a promotion, pay raise, new car,
and my own co-op house
Gone faster than a mouse
I finally would have reached the top
Guess I'm too independent and had to be stopped

ROLLING

Tumbleweed, tumbleweed, which way do you roll
Whichever way the wind blows

Found a job and apartment at a college in another city
Going back to school, the area is pretty
Choose the wrong department to get a job
Lose that on a general principle, head nod
At will state
At will sugar-coated racial hate
Head for the free counseling 'cause I don't know where to begin

Tumbleweed, tumbleweed, which way do you roll
Whichever way the wind blows
Keep school, lose my place
Now in a room
Still in counseling due to the gloom
Lose another job, and my unemployment too
GOD's breaking the ice around me
Frozen solid as can be
Dad dies—
No tears left to cry
More family goes
I'm not allowed to attend one of my grandmother's funerals,
no surprise
You don't want to know
A new church shines a light
Help with housing, so the tumbleweed stops its flight
No rolling for now maybe there's an end in sight

THE IN-BETWEEN

Had a dream my child came to me
I've come to set grandpa free
Wake up first hospital I call
Dad's there, he's not having a ball

When I call back
Nurse's attack
He only has two boys you don't exist
Me: Wait a minute is there something I missed?
Nurse: Well, his wife said that
Me: His wife is my mother
Nurse: You mean step-mother
Me: No, she gave birth to me
Nurse: Uhh, social work can handle this
I pray LORD there has to be a way
Can't deal with Mother and her issues
When I've got my own—not time for tissues

LORD provides
See my dad one last time
Funeral is a mess
It seems the ultimate test
One group of people I don't know, get in my face
Look good for a drug addict,
Where the rest your kids running tearing up the place
So may lies unravel at my expense

Another group who knows me well
Trying to get the truth to tell
Third group knows my dad
He's so proud of you

You always made his heart glad
Go back home and fall on my knees
Thank GOD, kiss the ground pleased
Then my partner in ministry dies—two days before my female surgery
Lung biopsies to check for another disease
Then more family members die
I never get the chance to say good-bye
Get another new church
Body breaks down and goes berserk
Lose one of my sister-friends
'Cause her wedding didn't happen,
and I'm too tired waiting for her to mend
GOD is purging me
With all the in-between

NOT CRAZY

Go to docs, can't stand up straight anymore
Doc says your body not happy with you more than some
Without doing test
Docs says body a mess
Test comes back
Doc confirms body under attack
Doc says:
Here's the list I've checked it twice
The big picture isn't nice
I'll do all I can, but surgery is eminent

As she talks, I'm trying to wrap this information around my head
I say:
You mean I'm not crazy
There really is something wrong with me
My illnesses are real
I'm not faking it pretending to be steel
Doc says:
No, it's real
When did this start
'Cause your body is falling apart

I say:
From the time I was a child
It started mild
Gotten progressively worse
In order not be hit or hear Mother curse
I learned how to fake it,
manipulate my body so it looks like I'm clumsy
or it was planned

Doc says:
Makes sense what you say

Your body is in pieces, now that won't stay
How do you want to proceed 'cause we got a fight
If your body is to get right
I say:
What are my options no one to take care of me
No options now for surgery

Doc say:
Braces to hold you up, physical therapy to strengthen
But surgery may not be a choice
An emergency to save your life
A lot of work to do

I say:
Okay, let's get to it
No time to play
I'm just glad I'm not crazy as everyone said
That broken record has played itself out in my head

GOD'S FIRST REVEAL

In this new church GOD does HIS first reveal
So I can see what's real
Pulls out my DNA so I can see
Exactly how HE's made me

GOD says:
There's a particular pace I created you to go
If your move faster than that you make mistakes
With decisions you weren't supposed to make
If you move too slow
Frustrates you more than you know
Only the things you do for Christ will last
But you must ask me first before the moment's passed
Or everything you do will be in vain
That's what adds to the unnecessary guilt, blame, and shame
Grow your roots in me
So you're unshakable as can be
Accept the pace I created you to go
The rest I promise to show

HEAVEN TOUCHED ME

Before the soul-journey could even begin
God had to first arrange a win
Four years before he started tearing down the house built on sin

For death, a major tragedy opened the door
Had happened four years before

Gradually, as grief came off of me
God began tearing up rooms and floors and I let him be

Every retreat I had started to take
God took out the garbage the world did make

Slowly, I became free to just be
On a Christian singles retreat
The Lord I did meet

Gazing upon the amazement of God's love
I really had no idea what was in store

Sitting, viewing mountains amazed as can be
I touched heaven—and heaven touched me

God made love to me earnestly
I sailed beyond ecstasy as HE penetrated me
Contented, satisfied I finally fell asleep
Now God can begin His operation and not be meek

THE LORD IS MY MASTER

The LORD is my master
HIM only will I seek after

The LORD is my master
That means HE knows what's best for me

The LORD is my master
HIS will, purpose have special meaning to me

The LORD is my master
How wonderful, how free

The LORD is my master
All means everything

The LORD is my master
He created wonderful, uniquely, me

The LORD is my master
That means Jesus set me free

A SOUL'S HOUSE DESTROYED

I discovered when I came back
There was nothing left of my house
Not even a tack

God cleaned me out that is true
Only thing left was the foundation, and it was shades of black and blue
The foundation that looked so cold
Was full of black and blue mold

God had a good construction crew
The workers took their work and flew

Up came my principles on money
That allowed me to attract the wrong honey

All of my identities came next
Boy did God know how to flex

School became God's distracting tool
As HE hit each pool

With no job, I didn't know myself
I had all these years put me on a shelf

With no money in my pocket, I thought I would die
Then someone with a little bit God would send by

No food to put on my table
How amazing to me that God was so able

For until their mistake was discovered
10 dollars in food stamps was my cover

Thankfully, I had clothes for my back
Even better—they weren't all black

Digging up my foundation, hurt like hell
I wanted God to sound the round ending bell

PURGE

Oh Lord, why am I so sick
I need you to make me well—quick

The Lord said in this weakened state
My power will be able to surge
So then my girl, you can purge

The next thing I knew
All sorts of thoughts, memories, and words flew

For every time I decreased
The LORD's power increased

Then when I felt a sudden urge
God once again said—PURGE

Up came stuff, some I already knew
Others were revelations new

Sometimes I knew what I said
Other stuff stayed in my head

I had no knowledge then
I couldn't stop couldn't say when

It was months later
I realized God did me a favor

Before I can have a heart that will merge
God knew I had to purge

THANK YOU IN ADVANCE

During the time of my being sick,
The LORD gave me another revelation real quick

Since two is better than one
The LORD revealed a ton

Be like that one leper, real sick
Who turned around and thanked the Lord real quick

Therein lies book number two
Describing and thanking God for that husband who'll appear
While God makes our hearts more clear

I have to be thankful right now
For I don't know when he'll blow into town

As I lay on my bed real sick
Odes to a husband came quick

For I'd had no idea if we had already met
God hasn't told me yet

As the tangled confused cobwebs that had been weaved
Suddenly, took their leave

And the sickness had run its course
And the voice that was once hoarse

Sleeping beauty started to arise
'Cause now she is coming alive

To God, most faithful and true
I thank you for that husband who won't make me blue
Because Lord I hold dearly, trusting and seeking in you

PURITY

Seven years of keeping my feet on the floor
The devil thought he could open a door

Men popped out near and far
Some on the bus, some by car

But for each one that I met
I yelled and screamed, "*Not yet!*"

Quite a few I had to put in their place
Making sure not to leave a trace

What make you think I'll chase a date
When I don't chase peas on plate

The more I became modest and pure too
The more men became unglued
I was real now, not a fake

Using God's discernment
He revealed the men who lust, therefore no trust

I refused to take their flack
Instead handing them smack right back

Only one struggled to hang in there true
Though I did my best to send him away too

But he admired my purity
He told me I'll get the best and him too

Purity comes with its own rewards simple and true
As I held on to my purity

God made me see
The changes HE's made in me

LOVE FLIGHT

Now that I've discovered God's love in flight
I can see much better in the light

For one headlight beam
Only gives over a gleam
While two cross over the other to show you the seams

I traveled a long time with only one light
I've walked into, and fell into, too many holes in the night
Now finally God's love has taken flight

As the Lord gathered in my supportive crew
For only the LORD knew

The more I discovered what was wrong
God sent those HE knew would help me be strong

For as I found myself
God took love off the shelf

Now I no longer have to fear the night
'Cause God gave me love in flight

SUPPORTIVE PEOPLE

Having supportive people in your life
Doesn't just mean a husband or wife

It means all types of people the good and the bad
Some make you happy, others make you sad

Having supportive people around you
Helps you grow in many ways too

Support isn't just finance
But mental, emotional, physical, and other ways
Just remember God is the one who makes them go or stay

Know it or not, you're their mission
Fulfilling the great commission

Some of them are armor bearers—mighty and true
They hold you up when you're weak, sad, and blue

Some in the devil they trust
They perform the growth that is a must

So don't get caught up in bitter and mean
Look to your support, God sent to help set you free

Utilizing God as your guide
He'll show you what's on their inside

Using the wisdom and discernment that GOD has provided
You won't get side tracked, bogged down or be misguided

911 GOD

It wasn't 'til after Dad died
That I fully understood why
GOD was out of place
It seemed there was no space
You see every time my dad did something for me,
Mother made him pay a price that filled her with glee
As GOD cleaned out the place that held my heart
So HE could give me a new start
I had to look back and see
What my dad meant to me
My dad wasn't in my sight
Mentally or emotionally, except for a fight
Physically he was always there
That's how I knew he cared
But I didn't have any value so I thought
Had to make it worthwhile, the price my dad bought
Which meant I had to do everything I could
If I couldn't win as I thought I should
Picked up the phone and gave my dad a call
He'd hurry to try and catch me after the fall
When in reality
I should have called before the decision was made
you see
Talk things out first with Dad,
then things wouldn't get so bad for me
Transferred my warped mind
To GOD in kind
Didn't call GOD first
Fought 'til I thirst
Then asked GOD to get me out the mess
Like studying the day of a test

As my life winds down,
Knew through GOD there was a different town
So GOD used to be my 911
That's starting to change—now hope has begun
So if your thoughts of GOD are bad
Look at the way your dad made you mad
'Cause Fathers are the reflection of GOD
They are what we see that gives us a nod
Problem is that reflection is not real
GOD isn't human that's the deal

TRANSITION

What an awful situation
To be awaiting your transition

As I sit and wait for a move
I find out it disturbs my groove

While I have joy
I feel like a toy

Waiting for God to let me be
And the devil to stop toying with me

Haven't I suffered long enough
I never asked for a whole lot of stuff

Isn't my faith deep
'Cause this hill is steep

How much more could I trust
I'm feeling an answer is a must

What more do I gotta do
'Cause this waiting is making me blue

All my favor appears to be long gone
Causing me to bemoan

Is this test just for me

Good grief the anticipation
As I wait for this transition

GOD NEVER PROMISED

God never promised
A rose garden, but a garden of thorns to build character

God never promised
Wealth beyond all measure of houses and gold on earth
But riches unbelievable in heaven

God never promised
An easy time on this earth
But persecution for the stand in him we take

God never promised
You the crop you sowed and reaped
But a cross to carry and death daily

God never promised
To supply all your wants
But only your needs to make it through today

God never promised
Tomorrow but today this second
This minute this hour

God never promised
Your fantasy and expectations to be fulfilled in man
But only HIS love that heals, provides, has peace
and gives joy

YESTERDAY LEADS TO TODAY

What happened yesterday leads to who you are today
What happened yesterday determines
your determination to leave or stay

What happened yesterday can make you,
or break you, if you let it
What happened yesterday was yesterday don't sweat it

What happened yesterday will either make you weak
or strong
What happened yesterday was neither right, or wrong

What happened yesterday determines the path
of your soul
And it's freedom to roam

What happened yesterday determines the journey
that your soul takes
What happened yesterday determines the hearts you break

EVERYTHING TEACHES

Everything, every relationship, every event teaches
It does it better than the Pastor preaches

While you're thinking how did "it" know
It was there to make you change and grow

The question becomes *were you paying good attention*
As you went through or suffered through the situation

Or did you ignore it, toss it, or let it pass by
While you hopelessly believed a lie

Instead of seeking after the truth
Before you drowned yourself in vermouth

Because everything shows you a different aspect of yourself
What you need to take off, or put up on a shelf

Everything brings some deficit you have to light
That you've been ignoring, because it hurts and feels too tight

Some things are to help you to discover the best parts of you
So you can save them for the rainy days that are shades of blue

So before you get upset with what Pastor preaches
Remember it is the situation you're in that teaches

YOU REMIND ME

You remind me of my new reality
That my days of walking on the beach hand in hand with someone
who loves me have passed me by
You remind me that my days are now more consistent of one
instead of some
You remind me that there is no one left just for me
That men are used up from trying to love someone who didn't love
them
or care
And now have no love or care left for me to share
You remind me that although I can no longer carry my burdens alone
I'm too old to have someone to share them with me like a wishbone
You remind me of memories and dreams that I used to have real sweet
That it's time to pack them in real neat
Yet I cling to the one-percent hope
That before my last breath maybe a man will still think I'm better than
dope
With my hard struggles to get by
Now alone I cry
Is there no other left, but sorrow's song
Was my pickiness so wrong
Is it really over, no hope left
I feel so bereft
Because unfortunately you remind me I'm not quite dead yet
Yesterday's song has not the future met

THE COMFORT OF A MAN

The comfort of a man is what I seek
Comfort isn't designed for the weak
A lap I can crawl into so I can be held tight
Words whispered, "It's going to be alright,"
Dealing with the stress and the pain,
Makes it seem like there's nothing to gain
Just some god with skin on
Not sex or bad behaving spawn

My counselor said:
You're missing your dad's lap as a seat
You're a woman, not a girl, who needs to stand on her feet
You're setting a man up for a fall
Especially if he has no self-control at all

I wasn't expecting that
Her answer took me aback
Some boulders lifted, and a few links fall off my chain
As I realize I'm not alone in the blame
Taking care of myself, I do the best I can
But it's all right to sometimes need a man

THE *L* WORD

He:

This can't be the *L* word so soon
The last one just took me over the moon

Gave her all I had
Yet she made me sad

The *L* word scares me to death
Like kryptonite to Superman, I'm allergic like meth

Yet holding her in a hug tight
Everything about this feels right

How can that be when I swore the one before was my last
How could I feel what I do so quick to forget the past

Fear keeps me from expressing myself
I only want comfort before I go on the shelf

She:

No way this is the *L* word after the last strong decoy
I still haven't figured out if his mission was to destroy

The *L* word has never been a part of my life,
Don't want anyone that close—too much strife

But something strange has been stirred up in me
'Cause seeing him fills my heart with glee

I wonder if he knows how much more scared I am than he

I don't dare hope, or hold my breath, but this feeling won't let me be

They:

He: No *L* word, not with all the pain it brings about
She: No *L* word, for it means nothing but scream and shout
They: Go away *L* word—don't put us in a pickle
'Cause *L* word, you're too fickle

He: No *L* word for I've love the wrong women to hard
She: No *L* word—for it means nothing, it's just something in a card
They: Go away *L* word we don't want you to stay
Please *L* word just go away

ULTIMATE REJECTION

Rejected since birth
Lost my only child who gave me five years of mirth

Now to my ears, I can't believe
Mother wants to visit for a week—no relief

How can this be
That it's me she wants to see

Rejected for as long as I can remember,
Rejected all the way 'til about two Decembers

As it is, no one really loves me
How can they when I have a mother who rejected me with glee

Too scared to let anyone get real close
Even those friends who say they care for me the most

If she comes and rejects me now
Does that mean I'll never have love 'cause I don't know how

What am I supposed to do
'Cause she'll be on my turf if she chooses to make me blue

How am I supposed to protect myself
God, where am I on this shelf

God says totally lean on Me
Me: I'm trying, but I have a mother who inflicts pain with glee

Calling on my prayer warriors now

'Cause I'm a basket case and how

She'll be heading here within a month and a half
Doing my best not to add this math

Pain that was ignored, finally kicking in
I cry all night depressed in my skin

Praying, God this hurts—remembering the past
God says, but you'll get the pain out at last

Finally writing everything down
I feel some relief, and I'm coming around

NO MORE ILLUSIONS

GOD swept up the pieces of my shattered heart
And the ice cracked that I was encased in
Melted as I watched the world's sin
Tears, I thought had finally dried
Rose to the surface threatening to fall
Counseling made me face the first layer of pain
Then the anger came
My mother's first visit I gave my Pastor Funeral arrangements
Thought she was coming to finish her job
Kill me, throw me in a ditch 'cause nobody would miss me and sob
When she left I just sat in a corner in a ball
Trembling refusing to take calls
Second year she came, I breathed
like a whale who had to release water through a spout
Tears started to come out
It seemed all I did was cry
Glad I had a counselor on hand
Four days with her I could hardly stand
Frustration and anger fly can't work or pay my bills
No one to care for me
GOD is this really your will

FLAT

'Tween the stress of dealing with Mother
Who took time to be bothered
It was like she finally discovered
That she had a daughter
Doing my best
To pass GOD's test
Finally, nothing worked
Braces, physical therapy, and walkers, my body still did its own jerk
When I could no longer stand
Surgery was a demand
Two years spent flat on my back
My emotions and mental state under attack
Only four friends to care for me
Not one person in my family
My most private struggle
Became a public dilemma to juggle
This church prayed for me
Not adding any more links to my chains with glee
Domino affect came
Docs said life for me won't be the same
Permanent damage of muscles and nerves
This is a sudden curve
Physical therapy was hard, and my instructors kept up with me
So I can go my own pace and be
Then one day the hairs on my neck stood up
Here comes **Midnight Blue** and his heifer sure enough
Laying eyes on him after so many years
Brought out a lot of my fears
GOD said look into his woman's eyes
The pain she can't disguise
That means nothing has changed

He blindsided her, being here was pre-arranged
I didn't even bother to guess
Who told him I was at my weakest
'Cause dealing with that,
means Mother's nice wasn't her squeakiest

COME AND GET THIS

Heifer come and get this
The pain in your eyes says **Midnight Blue** has not changed
Your life has been re-arranged

Heifer come and get this
He's one mistake I don't want to repeat
I remember being burned by that heat

Heifer come and get this
He took two lives from me
'Cause I wanted to be free

Heifer come and get this
Trust me, he's not something I'll miss
He's up to his same old tricks
Throwing the rock and run
Leaving you behind so he could watch the fun

Heifer come and get this
No need for you to watch me with hateful eyes
I'm not the one you need to despise
Can't you tell you've been tricked and lied

Heifer come and get this
'Cause if I start to again pray
You'll have to permanently go away

GOD come and get this
I don't need a repeat of hell
No change can't you tell

GOD come and get this
Tell me what to do to make him leave
No running behind him that promise I'll cleave

GOD said Forgive
And a new abundant life you'll live

No problem LORD from the hole in my heart
I'll forgive for a new start

When I turned again to my right
My instructor was standing in my sight
Putting his arms around me
Pulling me towards him free
When we go to the other side of the room
He half turned me to see the doom
The back of my ex's head was all I saw
But just in case he was waiting to follow me
I took the long way home so I can see
GOD said Don't worry you're safe and free

FORGIVE

GOD said
It's necessary to forgive
In order for men to live

Showing goodness, mercy,
and grace from heaven above
We must forgive and love
For all the past hurts and pain
Forgiveness is the only way to triple the gain

As GOD puts a cap, seal and throw out my past
I realize I'm free at last
For every person, place, and thing that had me blue
I forgave as JESUS said they knew not what they do

As my soul journey ends
I meet love journey in the bend
Welcoming, smiling, and glowing
I walk in purpose
and confidence with GOD the All Knowing

Nearing The END

Entering into a new decade of life
I willingly let go of the strife

An easier struggle ensues
The old struggle faded hues

Really looking at reality
Thanking God for me

New ideas, new dreams
A ton of blessings I'm ready to receive

God if it wasn't for you
What and where would I be and do

Thank you Jesus for a new outlook on life
No more drama, no more strife

An easier struggle now to endure
Pain and heartache will be no more

For I get it, really get it, you see
For it's not all about me

Put Jesus in front leading and guiding this life of mine
While I'm in back of God who shines

A new decade past, battles mostly won
Rebuilding, new foundations has finally begun

UPHEAVAL

The ending of any transition
Causes upheaval before the new position

Caught like a whirlwind and riptide
In limbo on the inside

Feelings confused and unsure
As I stand before the new door

Not sure if I want to go inside
Holding my breath before the door opens wide

What's behind this new door
If I stand too much longer I many never get to know

Am I really ready for this
Why do I feel there must be something I missed

GOD, you're drop-kicking me out
I want to stay wrapped around your leg I shout

As I make preparations for some of the new
There really is no time for shades of blue

Like a child on her first legs
I'm wobbly, and feel like a powder keg

Why can't I keep some of the old for support
They have a different path and will hold you back, the report

It's best if they support from a distance—afar

Just remember they got you here with my (GOD's) help thus far

Time for them to learn and stretch grab things new
Friends forever there'll be no shades of blue

Then why do I feel like something died
'Cause all of you grew on the inside

All of you have left something behind
That's why the upheaval, whirlwind, and riptide
Don't worry, all of you will adjust
Just not clinging to each other like dust

Are you ready to open that door now
Or stand there mooing like a cow

Okay let's do this although I'm so scared
Don't worry, it's me GOD who brought you here

With knees shaking and clinging to GOD's hand
GOD opens the door at my command

DIDN'T WANT TO KNOW
Mat 25: 31-46

To the people who scream *I didn't know*
Of course you didn't, you didn't care
You were never really there
Don't scream, that's not fair

The ones who sat on the ground full of mud,
holding on to a rope for dear life in rain, sleet, snow,
and all kind of weather
They refused to let go even a tether

Making sure I can still hear their voice
Though I was in a pit of darkness with a rope,
no light feeling like I had no choice

While you came to me with your fist full of accusations
and lies
Daring me to defend myself with disgust
and despise in your eyes

You didn't want to know the real truth
'Cause you didn't' want to support, love, or protect me
That's what all the bad people see
It's the real reason why I was under attack
'Cause they knew nobody had my back

Meanwhile, these people GOD gave to me
Did what they could to bring me out of the pit free

No you didn't want to know
Thinking by doing nothing,

you were teaching me lessons
Showing me I needed to be strong
In spite of the fact I had no knowledge of life and its wrongs

You didn't want to know I had never been taught
Everything that happened was not my choice,
but lies I had bought

You didn't want to go the extra step
To make sure my needs were met
Yet I gave all of you my last
When I let go and made you my past
Next thing I know I'm on blast

Amnesia sets in about all I did to help you
Forgetting myself, I allowed you to turn me blue
Finally, when I've had enough
Disappeared taking only my stuff
Next thing I know here come these lies
People in my face with accusations, disgust,
and despise in their eyes

No you didn't want to know
'Cause then you'd have to cover me, support me,
protect me, love harder than you can handle
That's why my life has to be dismantled

CROSSROADS

Standing, staring, at the division in the road
Sitting on what's left of the baggage I hold
A decision has to be made
Sun burning, needing shade
The one road wide enough for me
and the rest of my baggage
The other road just barely room for a cabbage
Bitterness, pain, resentment, loneliness, beg me to come on
A sweet smell, a mansion, jewels, sapphire, gold, joy, peace, love, say
heed the call
One road looks like it gets narrower with each step
The other grows wider, littered with broken glass, the glare my eyes
met
Narrow road
The past behind
The present stays current
The future always in sight
The Wide Road
The past consumes and overtakes the present day
The future gets further and further away

At a crossroads, a decision has to be made
Can't take bags on the narrow road
They will have to be left behind
The wide road I carry the bags, chains, boulders myself

Do I want to be chained, consumed 'til death forever be
Or do I leave it all behind,
walk what appears to be alone, but free
Swallowing hard
A last look at a card

With tears in my eyes
I stand, step forward with the chains—
Take a step toward the narrow road
I hear a **_CLINK_**
Look down, there's a break in the chain links
Instead of feeling the cold
That made me feel so old
There a warmth that melts the ice
Slow is the price
One more step I fall down
The weight is heavy all around
Suddenly I'm lifted in the air
I feel the arms of GOD who cares
With chains that rattle
Naked and tattered
A strong force of love
Swoops down from heaven above
Tail end of wilderness is ready to go through
Glad I chose this road and not the other one blue
It's not easy, it appears nothing has changed
But the broken links in the chains seem rearranged
In this life there are many crossroads on this earth
Many changes are given birth
Decisions have to be made
There's pain and there's gain
There's sun, and there's rain
There's lessons learned
There's bridges burned
The decision is yours to make
The right one there's less and less baggage to take
The wrong one the baggage comes along
Allows you to continue singing the same sad song
Both ends in death

But one resurrects to life
The other is permanent death and strife
The choice is always yours
Only the crossroads know the score
No matter what you do,
there's a crossroads in the way
It's not avoidable it will appear one day
The decision is up to you
Joy, or the shades of black and blue

HARVEST

Matthew 13:24-30
Isaiah 61: 2-3

Time for the Harvest to Begin
Sorting out reality grief doesn't win

REMEMBER

As I took the exit that GOD directed
GOD said:
There's something that needs correcting
Remember on that fateful day
When you were given a choice
I allowed you to give petition a voice
You asked that you live long enough to see your child's face
Hoping to die in his place
Then you said if he's to die
You wanted time to enjoy him in the by and by

Well your prayers were answered in several ways
'Cause he wasn't meant to stay
He lived to the age of division
Fulfilling his one mission
To keep you alive, to reach your strength
So you could leave the ball chain with extended length
His death has freed you
Like Christ did from sin
So you could evaluate and look deep within
You were also freed from another albatross
The man who was never your husband, but a boss
Actually more like a slave owner
With no benefits, he was just a loaner
No peace from them you would have
Bloodshed would be the bath
That washed you clean
From a people set out to be vindictive and mean
Press on, you've got a ways to go yet
Completely free you'll get
Cleaning the wounds and cutting the chain

Will definitely cause more pain
But if you press on towards the mark
Light will erase the dark
By my son JESUS' stripes you are healed
The Holy Ghost will comfort & seal
When you fulfill your purpose and give me the glory,
The truth will be your story
You'll lose if you forget how you made it through
And make the same mistakes too
As you leave this wilderness land
Don't forget the command
Remember

BROKEN CUP

I'm a broken cup put together with weak glue
It looks like I've bonded, but be careful I can still fall apart too
There are cracks that haven't broken yet
Once again be careful, don't get me wet
Even the handle that has been glued too many times
Is askew and crooked half hanging on, halfway tied
with glue that supposed to bind
There are gouaches and pieces taken out
No holes, still looks usable without a spout
I'm polished and shiny like new
Just don't look too closely, you'll see the glue
GOD comes along and shatters the cup
Time for a new one redesigned no doubt
Fashioned stronger,
better with the ability to hold more
GOD is certain, never more sure
A broken cup it will be no more
Instead, brand new,
with other abilities including a spout to pour
As it goes through the kiln, the fire much too hot
This cup will be perfect without a spot
As it sparkles all shiny and new
You can't touch it for it needs to cool too
Finally, when the process is done
GOD will let it be known HE has won
A brand new cup for GOD to fill
It overflows as it sits still

MY TIME

Lord is it really my time
To reclaim all that is mine
Am I ready for this
For the eternal joyful bliss
Will people be able to handle all that they see
Accepting even the unseen that is me
Am I Lord ready for this
Have I done everything—nothing missed
As I go through your finishing school
Make it clear what are my tools
As the time quickly approaches,
and I prepare
Keep me covered Lord, from your majestic glare
As people ask what do I say
As I approach the joyful day
Go before me Lord, with your grace and truth
As I follow your orders like Ruth
As my time approaches, I pray for nothing to go awry
For on that day joyful tears I'll cry
So GOD I'll gladly embrace my time
For you are the one my spirit binds

DÉJÀ VU

Have you ever been somewhere that reminds you of all the pain, all the
loss,
all the anguish you've been through
Have you ever looked around
and wondered why a place makes you so blue
Have you ever been somewhere
and seen all the red flags you missed before
Have you ever hesitated walking out your door
Have you ever fought so hard that's all you know how to do
Have you ever looked at things once, twice,
and blinked too
Have you ever come face to face with your past
Hoping hard that it won't last
Hearing every trick,
Watching the way people tick
Hoping, praying, that you're wrong
'Cause you don't want to sing a sad song
Hoping to take a good breath, exhale for once
Instead of holding it, waiting for that one drop
That pops the top
Tired frustrated, pissed
Feeling dissed
Wanting to cry
Doing too much to try
Not sure of where you belong
No longer wanting to go along
Losing sleep, hope
Wanting to give up
Understanding your situation ain't new
Wanting to hold on to you
Have you ever come face to face with your past

Finally looking at the turmoil at last
Hoping to find a trace
Of peace in that place
Not sure what you should do
Struggling to keep from being blue
Have you ever come face to face with the past
Have you ever been somewhere that reminds you
of the you that didn't last

HEART

What makes the heart beat so strong
Without first determining if it's wrong
With GOD did you check
Did the thought ever go above the neck
Is it a legitimate desire true
Or a deceitful one causing blue
Was the heart ever renewed
Or is there some dirt left in the cracks
The kind lightly scrubbing couldn't keep track
What if it's broken, shattered into pieces
A heart with no more creases
Or filled up with bitterness and hate
So full, there's no room for good to mate
Have we checked double, triple time
Before shouting Lord my heart is yours, not mine
Have you gone thru the process again
Only to be shown you can't begin
Not 'til you get rid of a thing or two
And to GOD be stuck like glue

ABILITIES

The things GOD created me to do
Not something people make me do
that created the shades of blue
The natural ease of things that can be done
For the kingdom won
Talents that allow GOD to shine
And cause us some time to whine
Sometimes requiring a swift kick in the pants
Drop-kicked into without romance
Justifying right for GOD that can't be outdone
For all the battles we can't see that are already won

WAIT

Wait, patience has engulfed you in a tight hold
Wait, for there is a miraculous joy to behold
Wait, for the anguish of it all will be soon be gone
Wait, for the ecstasy that will soon take over
Wait, for you are on standby
Wait, the days are gone that you cried
Wait, gone soon is the pain
Wait, comes the day of gain
Wait, soon will come the day you are free
Wait, for the sound of the chains breaking that enslaved thee
Wait, daybreak has come
Wait, the morning of the rising sun
Wait, night has finally gone by
Wait, for soon you can breathe a sigh
Wait, to GOD your heart must be true
Wait, these days are gone soon that were blue
Wait, for the breaking of the sky
Wait, purpose done you must say goodbye
Wait

THE END OF ME

Having no more fight
Waiting for darkness to turn to light
Feeling so battered, so black and blue
Struggling to GOD be true
No choice left, ordered to stay still
Succumbing to GOD's will
Sitting in a corner, hugging the wall tight
An angel stands and two others hover over me in flight
Usually in perpetual motion
Now still like a bottle of lotion
Empty, wrung out, weak
GOD reminds me the earth belongs to the meek
Having no more strength left
Tears flowing, silently wept
Waiting for GOD to tell me what to do
Doing my best to battle the shades of black and blue
Angels doing what they can to help me battle the pain
Life or death there will be gain
Coming to the end of me
One way or another the devil has to flee
Tucked in the corner of the heat
Watching GOD create a new heart that has a faint beat
Trembling, doing my best to stay still
Guarded, awaiting GOD's will

TODAY

Today Lord I give up
There is no more fight left within me
Today Lord
I make the decision to follow through with your plan
Today Lord
I turn it all to you get me out the mess as soon as you can
Nevertheless, not my will but yours, LORD I succumb
Today Lord
I ask, I plead, I pray,
for my steps to be ordered in that specific way
Today Lord
I ask for more—more faith, more love,
more wisdom, more discernment, more clarity
Today LORD
I ask for all of you and less of me
Today Lord

GOD'S SECOND REVEAL

In this new place recognizing some things like never before
Fighting the devil on a new level trying to score

GOD did a second reveal and said
When you left you were looking for the first
brick in the yellow brick road
Open your eyes, it's in front of you now that you
walked through the door
Boundaries are flexible fences that let out the bad,
and keep in the good
Time to set them, and protect them as you should

Everything you've been through springs from childhood and more
You see the devil's lost, and he's working hard to even the score

I created people in categories of beginning, middle, and end
This way you'll always need each other in life
especially to help you mend

Beginners are those who know how to get things started
Once things begin, they get broken-hearted
They need a middle and end person to keep them going
So they don't get lost in just sowing

Then there are the middle people, who love to work hard
They always need a project to help out with a nod
They need a beginner and an end, so they can keep on track
and know when to say when

Enders are finishers they get things done
They need a beginner and middle to say if they lost or won

There are several dialects in between
I won't go into it all 'cause we're dealing with you
So you can stay a peaceful blue

I also created you with a learning deficit too
Now that you know how you learn
It can't be changed, and you won't get burned

You also have a love language that is uniquely you
It's not love if they won't learn your language
You're not in love if you don't want to learn theirs

Now that you know how you were created
You can be a shining star
Fulfilling your purpose to the end
Once you're on the mend

You also know what to pray for
For each situation needs a beginning, middle, and end
Knowing how you learn,
lets you know how much time you need
So you can succeed
Then I can answer you exactly
Remember my timing is different from yours
Don't hold me to no exact time
For me (GOD) that's a crime

ASKING HOPING

What do you say to a mother
Who lives in total denial
That's she's the reason for all your trials
Judges are terrified of the files that they have to look at
Their world is entirely shook
For all the records show
That it's impossible to know
When this disability appeared
'Cause it means a mother never really cared
Judges keep looking, hoping it's not abuse
A child neglect, messes with their intellect
It's got to be workers' compensation
But she never stayed with one organization
Maybe it's medical mal practice
But there's no hospital record on the atlas
How about a sports injury
However, she never could climb a tree
Mother keeps asking, hoping
For someone else to blame
To admit it's *her*, makes her shame
For then she has no choice but to go back
To her own private attacks

Mother keeps asking, hoping
The conversation she never wants to start
So she talks for five minutes, scared to look at her own heart
Especially since there was never any support
She doesn't know about the first child I had to abort
Never could have any children, no room inside of me
Wasn't till my second child, the doctors made that plain to see
I did my very best, really tried
Yet and still the only one that lived—died

Mother keeps asking, hoping
That there is some other way to explain
I really don't know how to make it plain
How it is that my mother neglected me since I arrived
Yet somehow I managed to survive
When my child came, I tried yet he died
His death broke a circle of abuse
That really had no grounds for use
Before him his mother who came from that past
Was promised to never last
Her mother, the abuse was already spoken
Passed down like a broken subway token
At least one more generation before her
No one knows because it's a blur
If only the first one had the foresight to see
Three generations ahead to me
Maybe my child would still be here
It seems that no one cared

Mother keeps asking, she keeps hoping
For this disability issue to finally end
'Cause to look into her heart she doesn't think will mend
Seeing, dealing with all that pain
She's lost so much so sure there's nothing left to gain
When the truth is she'll free herself
So GOD could take her off the shelf
Then he could shower her with HIS LOVE
The permanent kind sent from up above
In the meantime, Mother keeps asking and hoping
I've resolved my issues no more misery
A piece of ice loosed from this frozen state of bondage
trying to get free

REPRESSED MEMORIES

Bits and pieces of a nightly nightmare
Each night the pieces unfold
Finally, the picture comes together
Like time and weather
It's like I'm there
Time has stopped nowhere to run, I'm stuck here
Reliving a major incident from my past
Pushed through my subconscious at last
Feeling every part of the emotion
That slathers all over me like lotion
All the anger all the pain
All the feelings of private shame
The yelling and screaming was the trigger
That froze me in place like a death rigor
Woke crying so hard
Couldn't catch my breath, pain coming in glass shards
Finally, come all that anger, pain, and emotions spent
I move, wash, dress my mind in a tent
Tired feeling sick, just moving is a chore
I pray I don't pass out on the floor
Gotta keep moving, work must be done
Three hours later, I swear I hear my bed yelling come
Mindless work didn't really help none
It hits me suddenly like a blast
Acknowledging the truth,
my dad should have taught me better comes at last
Maybe if he put his foot down and did more to protect me
I'd know the difference between bondage and free
So much to be reconciled about my life
So much pain, anger, and strife
If healing is ever to take place

The repressed memories have to hit you in the face
And everything that comes with it you must embrace
It's the only way to free yourself from the bitterness and pain
So that is more free ground that you gain
That's the meaning of taking your mind back
Each gain is a stronghold broken from the devils attack

AGONY

Lord please tell me you're still there
I need to know you still care
I understand this is something I need to do
Lord those shades of blue
Emotions and feelings for me are still new
Lord, I need to be held and set upon your lap
I need to burn this old bad map
A map I couldn't read
Going in so many wrong directions, and sowing bad seed
Lord, I know I got to praise you anyway
Good, bad, or ugly, just as long as you'll stay
I know what was evil will be turned to good
Everything is happening as it should
I need that peace that surpasses understanding
I know I'm not being demanding
These are your promises to me
As I struggle to break free

LOVE JONES

When I first saw your brother's face
It was you, not him, who took his place
Crying hard for 10 minutes at a time
I realized the secret hidden crime

Love Jones

Innocence lost, nothing left but shame
I took all the blame
Accepted love would never be my gain

Love Jones

Finally told, too many years too late
That you looked for me, blast fate
Man if I only knew back then
You'd now be sitting in my den

Love Jones

You were lied to, tricked and deceived
That I didn't care you believed
When just the opposite was true
I'm sorry for your shades of blue

Love Jones

Too late to turn back the hands of time
How I wish I knew about that crime
Looking at the ghost on his side of the bed
Could that have been you instead

Love Jones

You were the sun in my gloomy days
But it was so dark, I didn't feel the warmth, no way
How I wish I could go back now
Too late, we're two different people anyhow

Love Jones

You were a boy and I was a girl
Too many things made my mind whirl
I'm so sorry that you were made blue
If I'd known I'd have been true to you
My child gave love a start
But you'll always have a place
next to his in my new heart

Love Jones

Well GOD is calling me now
Letting go the last piece of my heart goes *POW*
GOD says it's time to let you go
So I can embrace the one HE's gonna show
If there really is one made for me
GOD provides the joy, he'll provide the glee

Love Jones

All these years I looked for a second chance
With a glimmer of romance
To have my final dance
Farewell forever my unrequited love
I'll see you in heaven up above

Love Jones

BREATHE

Every second of breath is lost time
It's spent before you know it was never truly mine
Just like breath, it's gone never to return
Things that happen are quick or long burns
So much to think about
You waste breath when you shout
Best to breathe slow
So you can feel the rhythm and flow
My pace was never to move fast
When I do I make bad decisions that last
Like breathe in small spurts
I need time to think, or else I get hurt
It's like moving opposite the earth
I'm traveling backward to birth
Exhaled breath freezes in the cold
Time lost, rots like mold
No matter what you do, like breath you can't get it back
Time is either GOD's or the devil's weapon of attack
If it's GOD's you could be pardoned
So you can be redeemed
Taking back what the locust ate
Blessing so abundant can't fit on a plate
If it's the devil's seeds of bitterness, anger, resentment, and hate
Take root like seeds growing with matching mates
Each breath is time spent
If you're not careful, you'll wonder where it went

TRADING ASHES

Before you trade your ashes for beauty
You must do a review
Looking out on my own town
I finally realized everything is burned to the ground
I'd been sitting in ashes all this time
So long the ash was ready to turn to lime
With tears pouring out my eyes
I realize it's time

Had to grieve for every single loss
Evaluate the damages and the cost
Start accepting those things that I cannot change
Everything else had to be rearranged

Some things were burned beyond recognition, had to go to trash
Others were salvageable, but I knew they wouldn't last
Taking inventory meant scraping out debris
That's when the last scream came out of me

LAST LAYER

Peeling off the layers of the onion,
I went through that first set of anger and pain
But this layer hit the center core, and it rained
It's the pain of that day, that second, that minute, that hour,
that couldn't be expressed
Like a giant infected pimple turned into a cyst,
it was a mess
All I could do was scream
Hitting a higher note than the Supremes
The ones who knew me best took note
'Cause they knew how long to let me stay under the bed
Before they came to check me out
After all, they were the ones who sat in the mud
and pulled me out

Those who don't know me well it was easy to tell
'Cause they were the ones who came unglued
Like being stuck in an elevator in darkness and gloom
They ran around to anyone in town thinking I was gonna die
When I had to scream 'cause I couldn't cry

It hurt too badly for water to come out of my eyes
Those who knew me best,
remember when I was flat on my back
The pain would come suddenly so tough I'd sit up in bed
with a silent scream from the attack

No words came out, not even a shout
But once it was over
I'd fall back to bed and back to sleep again
There was also the time pain would shoot me up out a chair

I'd hobble out the door to walk it off, acting like I need air
This scream was more intense
'cause I relived the horror of that day
That my enemies came out to make me pay
Left me for dead before they went away
Feelings I never knew I had ranging from sad to mad
I finally cried like I never had
It took a week,
and then some to process the majority of the pain
Once the infected part was out,
my friends helped me to see the gain
It took a year to handle every emotion that came out
I was a mess,
but my friends past the test, and gave me the room
I needed to vent and shout
They helped me to mend

With that scream, I moved from GODs intensive care down to critical
care
Apologized to those who don't know me,
and my friends who said
That I was putting it kind
If it had gone on much longer,
an institution they would find

But we love you to help you mend
I appreciate the fact GOD gave me friends
Each day I grow stronger
The past doesn't stay real long
As I get out my system all the wrong

FEELINGS

Discovering feelings that were new to me
Helped me see how I came to be
Always told feelings were really bad
I didn't know happy, mad, or sad
I wasn't free to discover love
Even the love from Heaven above
In the autumn of my life, in the night, bad dreams
Show me how my life fell apart at the seams
A boy I really liked and wanted to be true
I was scared for him so I turned him blue
If you loved me my mother made you pay a price
She added lies with lots of spice
Overwhelming feeling of abandonment, made me feel lost
I thought life wasn't worth the cost
All these years I was alone
Never had anywhere I could call home
Feeling pain so great
I married men full of hate
Having GOD as a spare key
I didn't know GOD came first you see
Nothing but hell in the pain
Didn't know there was better to gain
Not understanding GOD's power
My moods changed every hour
I was good at acting happy and fake
No one knew I was on the edge about to break
Pushing feelings down deep inside
Till they started coming out, nowhere to hide
So much I wish I knew
Maybe I wouldn't have so many shades of black and blue

RED

That's the color I see
When I review all that's happened to me
Finally thawed out enough
To truly understand the stuff
Told I had no feelings for anything with good dealings
Hard, crusty, abandoned
Daily in pain
Teased mercilessly
Told I'm stupid, ugly, colored so many shades of black and blue
Never knew what it was like to be a child
Loved, free, dreaming
Always faking the funk
Treated like a skunk
The layers are gone
Somehow, some way, I came out strong
Leaning on GOD
Frozen for a time
Feeling the pain
Embracing the hurt seeing the color red
So much anger to kill dead
The color burns out
I can shout and get past
Hold on to GOD who can last
Discovering that forgiveness has depth
It's not a surface thing that heals the rift
As you forgive, you forget the sting,
the pain, the way you felt
The hand you were dealt
You heal in a way
That only GOD has the say
Taking that broken, shattered, heart-piece

GOD starts to build the mosaic
That becomes the beginning of a new heart
One that has traces of lines and no start
The corner stone was set
Each broken heart-piece that heals the requirements met
Letting go freeing yourself
With GOD the cornerstone Himself
The color red starts to look outta site
Glowing, burning, day and night
'Til at last it burns out all the impurities
Knowing that life has no guarantees

GOD is pleased with red
The color of fire, blood, and what's dead
Because in death comes the life that was meant to be
The blinders gone, the weight lifted so finally I can be FREE!

WIDOWED

Ten days before I went back to work
A message from Ebony Black gave me a jerk
Now what does he want after all these years
Remembering the night of the seven-hour fight brought to surface tears

I don't need to be found, nor do I want him back
Fresh in my mind was that last attack
My bones brittle and black
All I could think of was how do I make him go away
LORD please, tell me he won't stay

LORD said
You must process this for you to forgive
You're on life support, a shock to your system, but you'll live

I said
LORD all the many lies that he told
Loud, big and bold
Another one who took advantage of a bad situation
Using his title for a propitiation
As usual, no one listens to me
As hard as I tried to be free

LORD said
What are the lessons you finally learned
you will never again be burned

I said
Learned to never make any decisions when I'm under too much stress
Run real fast from men who act a mess
If the man won't leave me alone

I can have my space to groan
Then report him right away
The police won't make him stay

LORD said
That's good enough, ready to forgive without fluff

I said
Yes LORD
I forgive, so I can live

Thirty (30) days later I get a new message
It said
This isn't who you think it is
And it's not a quiz
You see I wanted to let you know
Ebony Black is dead
I thought to his funeral you'll go

I said
Why on earth would I do that
When no memory of him for me was any good
I thought that was understood
Especially when I don't know what lies were told
All big and bold
Anything he left you can have
Don't want something that will be a curse
'Cause memories of him I don't want to nurse

The messenger said
Sorry to have contacted you then
Didn't mean to stir up memories of when

LORD thank you for setting me free
I'm a widow now, because of THEE

SLOW CHANGE

Accepting never a bride covered, cherished,
respected, always rejected
Keeping my head down
Faking a smile when I want to frown
Slowly picking my head up
Smile, slow, real, genuine like a pup
Beginning to enjoy those things
That life brings
A friend, a sister, a brother with no strife
Making flexible plans
Knowing GOD has my life ran
Making steps toward the purpose
HE created me to have
Moving when GOD does no need to do the math
Life suddenly seems rearranged
As I embrace the slow change

GOD'S DESIRE

GOD's desire
As I go through the fire
The Yearning
Burning
Love
Respect
Compassion
Flavor
Taste
Melting two into one

The sensual
Life finally begun
Outreach
So many to teach
Passion to save one
No matter what happens is better than none
And so much more is the gain

The abuse
Rejection
Misuse
Loss
Being tossed
Being beaten
Going through the motions
Never belonging

The game
Shame
Blame

GOD is going to use all that pain
Turn something good from all that bad
Using all the things that made me so sad, so mad
To help and heal someone else find their glad

GOD's desire melts into my own
Maturing, slowly become grown
Still very much that child
That was never wild
Struggle to breathe
Struggle to be
GOD knows what's best for me
Moving forward, shaking with each step
The Ice melts adds pep
Tears shed
No longer wishing to be dead
Starting to want to live
GOD's desire forgive
The giving of ultimate love
That started from heaven up above

GOD's desire
Becomes my fire
It warms the body
It frees the soul
Different tears I cry
The pain of the past says a long goodbye

GOD's desire
I embrace it as it starts to flow through my heart wire
Each shattered heart-piece
As it heals, becomes a jigsaw puzzle to be put together again
In a different way

With a different say
As I await the outcome
I can see what I was and what I can become

GOD's desire
An all-consuming fire
It burns so bright
Not consuming me, but taking out the fight
Pliant
Moldable
Taking shape
Creating something new
Joy replaces the shades of black and blue
Becoming my own
GOD's desire

MENDING

As the ice melts, it's easy to see all the pieces that need mending
Shattered heart-pieces that have been bending
Wilted, broken, out of shape
Put together with tape
Old, worn, disintegrated glue
A mess that needs to be made new
Some heart pieces need to be broken again
So it can heal up right
A broken mess that had a long night
A struggle to survive
Doesn't leave much to thrive
But now the mending has finally begun
Another round that death has not won
Healing is slow, but steady and sure
GOD works on what has gone before
Frozen and broken on a shelf
I finally start to find myself

BALANCE

What's done is done
In life there is no such thing as *do-over*
Finding myself, I find balance
Making sure GOD is first
So this way I am provided for and do not hunger or thirst
All the shuda, cuda, wuda, helps no one at all
The best thing is to take note
Of the lessons learned when you fall
A second chance always comes
It will be with someone different from the past
If you apply the lessons that will last
That's the scale of balance weighing in on life
For everything you do there will always be a price
GOD has given me mothers, sisters, and brothers who really care
Most of the time all I had to do is think and they were there
GOD also gave me fathers to add to the pie
'Cause HE knew mine had said good-bye
I have an uncle and an aunt, and even some of the cousins coming
around
Sad to say it isn't until you go through
That you learn how to play
Life sometimes can be that way

TEST DRIVE

I got a date for a test drive
Same day I ended a class to pick up my pieces
A man arrived

Reacting first out of fear,
I said can't go there
Then ran as fast as I can

GOD I'm not ready, no money for dinner or cab
Still not released to drive a car
I can't go out with a man
GOD said
This ain't about you
But the lessons that you learned
Do you remember what to do so you won't get burned

Thinking, and going over all my notes in my head
This is what **I said**
I remember when GOD wants to bless you HE sends a relationship
When the devil wants to curse you he also sends a relationship
Okay first question:
Did you GOD send this man
Second:
A request that reveals to me who this man is and what he is about

GOD's answer
NO, I didn't send this one and per your request this is who he is

I said
Okay so why must I go on a date if this ain't it

GOD said

Once again, it ain't just about you
I need to show you I got your back
I've got you protected, you won't catch an infection
You don't need material things,
For the one I have for you will give you wings
You need to feel comfortable, and know that I will show you the truth
when you ask
This is the lesson you need to grasp

So with GOD's notes in mind
Went on the date in kind
GOD had my friends near
Just in case something went wrong
Doing things this way helped me be strong

The man ruined his chance because he couldn't tell the truth
Amazing how he didn't figure out that I already knew
What he is
General questions he couldn't answer
A sure warning sign

I also knew that GOD was trying to teach him something too
Told my friends definitely he wasn't the one
We couldn't even be friends
'Cause his own agenda was what he wanted done

Doing things GOD's way meant
I didn't waste my time
Get distracted and lose my place in line

It don't take much when you want to help
The Key ask GOD FIRST to know if you should

He'll let you know and then you can follow through
So you're provided for
And the devil can't score

It's the autumn of my life
Must apply the lessons learned well
This keeps down the drama and strife
The same mess won't repeat or tell
From GOD's critical care
now on to GOD's stability
Trusting GOD more instead of me

FOUND MYSELF

Found myself
No longer sitting on a shelf
I know who I am
My purpose, GOD's plan
GOD's pace HE wants me to go
Boundaries set in place
Backup plan when broken to replace
What it is GOD wants from me
Heaven's glory mine to see
At peace to live life abundantly
Accepting the truth about my reality
Moving forward in totality
Not perfect, let's not go there
Just enough patience to spare
My wounds are signed and sealed
JESUS blood the devil can't appeal
All of my chains are broken and removed
GOD's rehab to get continually improved
Joy a plenty and praise
For my JESUS, my GOD and Holy Spirit
I raise
Found MYSELF

READY

It's the autumn of my life I'm ready
Moving along steady
The Holy Spirit is my permanent IV
JESUS continues to heal me
GOD comes first
No longer do I thirst
Made it to stable care
Wisdom kicking in so I won't go back there
Life is brand new
A comfortable shade of peaceful blue
GOD's eye on me Life swept
GOD's promises are kept

NO APOLOGY NEEDED

I'm not expecting an apology from you
Why?
Because I'm your biggest failure, ultimate mistake,
albatross around your neck, greatest curse
An apology from you I can't nurse

You've burned my bridges before I could even get to them
Why?
Because I wanted to be free, maybe some stability,
love, care, concern, a mother, a father, a career, children,
If I wait for an apology from you—I'll burst

'Cause even if you apologize, it won't be public, but secret
Why?
Because all those lies you told
are like feathers thrown off the highest building
You can't get them back

Nobody will believe me
when I publicly display all your attacks
Even with proof in black and white
I'll be thrown into a dungeon out of sight
Why?
Because they never saw your monster, the ruthless,
ugly, vindictive, mean of your reality
All they see is the dream of who you are
The one polished, humbled, without a wound or scar

NO, an apology is not needed
Not by me, because by the Grace of GOD
I've come too far
To be stuck, mummified,
dead bones of a skeleton in one place

The place that leads to nowhere, jail, a mental institution,

stone cold out of my mind
I'm putting it mild and kind

Besides GOD is the one who can reach you where you live
All I gotta do is Forgive
NO, no apology is needed

I'm grateful that to GOD only I have heeded
Which means I can let you be
'Cause that means that I have my mind,
stability, purpose
And FREE

SURVIVOR'S JOURNEY

The journey of a survivor is long and hard
It can't be done with a card
You have to revisit the past
To get untangled from the web of lies
Also to take off the disguise
Not everyone makes it to the end
'Cause you have to get through the pain to mend
It can't be done apart from GOD
Because relapses can happen with a nod
Life isn't a do-over—one chance, one shot
It's all you got
Holy Spirit does the work
You must be willing to make the decision to forgive
A more blessed and peaceful life you'll live
Don't expect or wait for your abusers to confess
You'll find yourself stuck in your mess
Don't expect an apology or change
It's a trap your life won't get rearranged
Sometimes reconciled means to let go
Accept your reality, because life isn't a nightly show
Keep yourself in GOD
So you won't get tricked into turning back at the devil's nod
Remember GOD takes care of things HIS way
Tomorrow is not promised, you only have today
Never want something so bad you'll do anything to get it
'Cause it's an idol that will get you destroyed
You'll be the devil's favorite toy
Hold to the faith and be true
GOD will take care of you
Returning to a peaceful shade of blue

ADDENDUM

If the first date started with a slap in the head a woman (man) wouldn't go out with that person again. It doesn't first you are given what they think you need to suck you in. Like a spider builds a web in order to trap flies. Wine, dine, offers of assistance, being there when you need them with one exception the occasional temper flare at someone else (waiter, waitress,) or you, followed by the apology. Then isolation of you from others your friends, family if they are important in your life, in my case there wasn't anyone. When the mind games stop working and the manipulation doesn't work they bring in their own supporters, friends, family who will then back them in their wrong. When that doesn't work then the hitting starts, in my case I hit back so that was out.

When I was coming up there wasn't any protection for women. Domestic Violence shelters were death traps where you waited for your abuser or someone else's abuser to show up and shoot up the place or throw motive cocktails.

Orders of Protection were not enforced, people just stood and watched you get beat down and of course it was your fault. If you hadn't did what you did, or if you had did what you were told are just a couple of excuses.

The Stalker Law wasn't in effect until the 1990's. There wasn't any education for women on abusers or what to do or how to escape.

The stalker law
1)United States[edit]

The first state to criminalize stalking in the United States was California in 1990[50] as a result of numerous high-profile stalking cases in California, including the 1982 attempted murder of actress Theresa Saldana,[51] the 1988 massacre by Richard Farley,[52] the 1989 murder of actress Rebecca Schaeffer,[53] and five Orange County stalking murders, also in 1989.[52][54] The first anti-stalking law in the United States, California Penal Code Section 646.9, was developed and proposed by Municipal Court Judge John Watson of Orange County. Watson with U.S. Congressman Ed Royce introduced the law in 1990.[54]

[55] Also in 1990, the Los Angeles Police Department (LAPD) began the United States' first Threat Management Unit, founded by LAPD Captain Robert Martin.

Within three years[54] thereafter, every state in the United States followed suit to create the crime of stalking, under different names such as *criminal harassment* or *criminal menace*. The Driver's Privacy Protection Act (DPPA) was enacted in 1994 in response to numerous cases of a driver's information being abused for criminal activity, with prominent examples including the Saldana and Schaeffer stalking cases.[56] [57] The DPPA prohibits states from disclosing a driver's personal information without permission by State Department of Motor Vehicles (DMV). As of 2011, stalking is an offense under section 120a of the Uniform Code of Military Justice (UCMJ).[58] The law took effect on 1 October 2007.

"Stalking is a controversial crime" because a conviction requires no physical harm.[59] The anti-stalking statute of Illinois is particularly controversial. It is particularly restrictive, by the standards of this type of legislation.[60]

1)http://en.wikipedia.org/wiki/Stalking

Family forget it, they couldn't help, wouldn't help or made things worse. Mothers who abuse their children don't realize that the lies they tell to get over burn the bridges a child needs to get the help, education and protection they need to make it in life.

It's because of women who died or survivors who lost children that Domestic Violence moved into the federal and state realms. Shelters have been upgraded with security to protect those who manage to escape. Classes on life training, money management, counseling and more are now provided for women of domestic violence. Children are now coming with the parent who has been abused. There was a time when the children had to be left behind. Those children are grown now and believe their mother didn't love them and left them deliberately which is not true. Before 2000 a woman couldn't escape with the children if she didn't want to be found or if she didn't want her children taken from her. You had to know someone who knew someone who knew someone in order to escape with the children without being found.

Listed below are definitions of a few ways a person can be abused. It is being discovered that there may be as many as thirteen different types of abuse.

2) Emotional Abuse
- Frequently blames or criticizes you
- Calls you names
- Ridicules your beliefs, religion, race class or sexual preference
- Blames you for "causing" the abuse
- Ridicules/makes bad remarks about your gender
- Criticizes or threatens to hurt your family or friends
- Isolates you from your family and friends
- Abuses animals
- Tries to keep you from doing something you wanted to do
- Is angry if you pay too much attention to someone or something else (children, friends, school, etc.)
- Withholds approval, appreciation or affection
- Humiliates you
- Becomes angry if meals or housework are not done to his/her liking
- Makes contradictory demands
- Does not include you in important decisions
- Does not allow you to sleep
- Repeatedly harasses you about things you did in the past
- Takes away car keys, money or credit cards
- Threatens to leave or told you to leave.
- Checks up on you (listens to your phone calls, looks at phone bills, checks the mileage on the car, etc.)
- Tells people you suffer from a mental illness
- Threatens to commit suicide

- Interferes with your work or school (provokes a fight in the morning, calls to harass you at work, etc.)
- Minimizes or denies being abusive
- Abuses your children
- Breaks dates and cancels plans without reason
- Uses drugs or alcohol to excuse their behavior
- Uses phrases like "I'll show you who is boss," or "I'll put you in line"
- Uses loud or intimidating tone of voice
- Comes home at late hours refusing an explanation

Financial Abuse
- Makes all the decisions about money
- Takes care of all financial matters without your input
- Criticizes the way or amounts of money you spend
- Places you on a budget that is unrealistic
- Prohibits your access to bank accounts and credit cards
- Refuses to put your name on joint assets
- Controls your paycheck
- Refuses you access to money
- Refuses to let you work
- Refuses to get a job
- Refuses to pay bills
- Causes you to lose your job

Sexual Abuse
- Pressures you to have sex
- Pressures you to perform sexual acts that make you uncomfortable or hurt you
- Directs physical injury toward sexual areas of your body
- Puts you at risk for unwanted pregnancy or sexually transmitted diseases
- Withholds sex or affection

- Calls you sexual names ("whore", "bitch", etc.)
- Tells anti-woman jokes or demeans women verbally/attacks your femininity or masculinity
- Accuses you of having or wanting sex with others
- Forces you to have sex with others
- Threatens to disclose your relationship when you did not want it known
- Forces you to view pornography
- Pressures you to dress in a certain way
- Disregards your sexual needs and feelings about sex
- Accuses you of being gay if you refused sex (for heterosexual relationships)
- Spreads rumors about your sexual behaviors
- Forces you or refuses to let you use birth control
- Makes unwanted public sexual advances
- Makes remarks about your sexual abilities in private or in front of others
- Rapes and sexually assaults you

Using Children
- Makes you feel guilty about your children
- Uses children to relay negative messages
- Uses children to report on your activities
- Uses visitation to harass you
- Threatens to take custody of your children
- Threatens to kidnap your children

Physical Abuse
- Pushes, grabs or shoves you
- Slaps you
- Punches you
- Kicks you
- Chokes you

- Pinches you
- Pulls your hair
- Burns you
- Bites you
- Ties you up
- Forces you to share needles with others
- Threatens you with a knife, gun or other weapon
- Uses a knife, gun or other weapon
- Prevents you from leaving an area/physically restrains you
- Throws objects
- Destroys property or your possessions
- Drives recklessly to frighten you
- Disregards your needs when you are ill, injured or pregnant
- Abuses you while you are pregnant
- Forces you to abort or carry a pregnancy

2) http://www.cdh.org/medical-services/services-A-Z/emergency/do-mestic-abuse/abusive-behavior-checklist.aspx#Emotional_Abuse

Domestic Violence starts subtle. At first you feel honored that the person asked you asked out. You don't think about how they got your phone number, knew where to find you or the reason why they asked you out on a date. They start with your mind. That outfit doesn't look good on you, you don't really like that, I know what is best for you. In marriage it's the perceived duties of a wife. Abusers usually surround themselves with people who will enforce the abuse from family members to friends. If they sound too good to be true there is a problem. If they have too much personal information about you (your work schedule, school schedule, your route home, etc) there is a problem. Don't over analyze everything; just pay attention to the red flags and your gut. I didn't know to do either or. By the time I paid attention it was too late and I thought I was stuck until I could figure a way out. In the autumn of my life I finally have the protection, care and concern that I need to feel safe to go out on dates. I have learned to ask GOD first and HE will reveal. You think you don't have time, trust and believe me when I say when it comes to your life; you should have all the patience in the world to wait for the right person to enter into your life. Get a life of your own, discover a hobby that keeps you interested, travel, cultural events (opera, ballet, etc), go back to school or take a class in anything. Explore you, discover you.

If you have read this book and you see yourself and you don't feel safe here are some numbers to call:

Domestic Violence
1800 621 4673
www.safehorizon.org
Sextrafficking
1888 373 7888
www.polarisproject.org
Runaways
1800 RUNAWAY
www.1800runaway.org
If you have read this book and you recognize someone you know ***Please*** use the above numbers.
Prayerfully this book has assisted someone.

With the Support of

Sojourner Center
Overcoming the Impact of Domestic Violence One Life at a Time

a Book's Mind

Whether you want to purchase bulk copies of
Shades of Black and Blue
or buy another book for a friend, get it now at:
www.abooksmart.com

If you have a book that you would like to publish,
contact Jenene Scott, Publisher, at A Book's Mind:
jenene@abooksmind.com.

www.abooksmind.com